Channel 4 and the British Film Industry, 1982–1998

Channel 4 and the British Film Industry, 1982–1998

Laura Mayne

Edinburgh University Press is one of the leading university presses in the UK. We publish academic books and journals in our selected subject areas across the humanities and social sciences, combining cutting-edge scholarship with high editorial and production values to produce academic works of lasting importance. For more information visit our website: edinburghuniversitypress.com

Edinburgh University Press Ltd
13 Infirmary Street
Edinburgh EH1 1LT

First published in hardback by Edinburgh University Press 2024

Typeset in 12/14 Arno and Myriad by
IDSUK (Dataconnection) Ltd,
and printed and bound by CPI Group (UK) Ltd, Croydon, CR0 4YY

A CIP record for this book is available from the British Library

ISBN 978 1 4744 3727 1 (hardback)
ISBN 978 1 4744 3728 8 (paperback)
ISBN 978 1 4744 3729 5 (webready PDF)
ISBN 978 1 4744 3730 1 (epub)

Contents

Illustrations

Acknowledgements

To Justin Smith, my supervisor, and my inspiration, I will be forever grateful that you attributed my jittery flailing during my PhD interview to enthusiasm rather than to the six espressos I had mainlined before meeting you. To Paul McDonald, whose advice and excellent eye for detail made the work immeasurably stronger. I am eternally grateful to everyone in the research department at Channel 4, and particularly Rosie Gleeson. Thank you to all the interviewees who so kindly provided their time. To my fellow Channel 4 project researchers Rachael Keene and Ieuan Franklin, for their patience and kindness, and for their forbearance about my tendency to keep Pot Noodles in our office filing cabinet. I can assure you that my diet has since improved. I am grateful to Michael O'Neill, my fondest and most sarcastic friend, and to Sally Shaw and Simon Hobbs, whose respective cheer always brightened the corridors of Portsmouth University on the dullest days.

Introduction

'We don't just show great films: we make them, too.' With this declaration in a 2014 advertising campaign, Film4 sought to establish itself to audiences as a producer of films as well as a curator of film culture. From its earliest days Film4 has operated as both financier and tastemaker, funding or co-funding between twelve and twenty films per year and importing films though its 'Film on Four International' broadcast strand.[1] While most readers will be familiar with Channel 4 as a funder and a curator of film programming in various guises, its film-funding and commissioning activities have been grouped under various titles over the years: Film on Four (from 1982–1998), Film Four (from 1998–2002) and finally, Film4 (2003–present). This book will weave a long history of the channel's involvement with British film culture, highlighting its relationships with key directors, producers and companies. The aim of this book is to place Channel 4's film financing initiatives in the context of the British broadcasting ecology by presenting a general historical overview which will examine the channel's relationship with British film culture in the 1980s and 1990s.

Channel 4 has historically been a source of significant support for the British film industry, acting as a consistent source of funding for producers at times of industrial decline, and changing the ways in which films have been financed and distributed in the UK and abroad. Channel 4 has funded films that have become synonymous with popular British cinema, as evidenced by the popular appeal and scholarly appraisal of films like *The Crying Game* (1992), *Four Weddings and a Funeral* (1994), *Trainspotting* (1996), *12 Years a Slave* (2013) and *The Favourite* (2018), to name just a few. For these reasons, it is particularly surprising that there has been no comprehensive study of Channel 4, its impact on the British film industry and its history as an institution. But the purpose of this study is not simply to bridge the gaps in the historical record. By focusing in detail on working practices in the television and film industries and how these have changed over time as a result of the channel's involvement, this book sets out to engage with questions about the nature of creativity, commercialism and cultural policy in television and film.

The book is organised into four sections, with each section focused on exploring Channel 4's relationship with the British film industry as a broadcaster of film, as a funder/producer of films for theatrical exhibition, as a talent house and, lastly, as a commissioner of films for international audiences. The focus throughout this book is on Channel 4's activities from 1982–1998, the period when the channel commissioned films through its Drama Department for broadcast on television via the 'Film on Four' strand and for (occasional) theatrical release in UK cinemas. The ethos and aims of the channel's film commissioning ambitions during this period is distinct enough from later eras in the channel's history to merit detailed consideration. In 1998 the channel's film production and distribution activities, which had diversified considerably throughout the 1990s, were merged into a standalone company – FilmFour Ltd – under the leadership of Paul Webster. Whereas Film on Four had previously employed a cultural policy towards film which was accompanied by a significant amount of economic security, FilmFour was a largely commercial enterprise which focused to a much greater degree on securing international co-production deals. Following the collapse of this venture in 2002, film sponsorship activities were subsumed within the channel once more, under the title of 'Film4'.

Part 1 explores the development of Channel 4's policy towards film during its early days as a broadcaster, and offers a detailed overview of a moment in British history which saw the forging of an unprecedented relationship between the UK's film and television industries. Chapter 1 focuses on the development of the channel's film-funding policies, while Chapter 2 explores the channel's corporate structure as a 'publisher broadcaster' and offers a detailed overview of the channel's commissioning processes from the perspective of both Commissioning Editors and the independent producers who were working to create programming in the rapidly expanding sector which was created almost overnight by the channel's arrival. Part 2 focuses on the early films commissioned by the channel for the Film on Four strand, as well as examining the complications that were created by the channel's ambition to secure UK theatrical releases for Film on Four productions. Chapter 3 deals with an academic debate which has today lost much of its relevance in an era of media convergence, but which is no less relevant to any account of the channel's history: the issue of whether television-funded films really can be considered to be 'cinema'. Chapter 4 considers the output of Film on Four in the 1980s and 1990s through the lens of film scholarship and analysis, situating Channel 4-funded films within the broader aesthetic and cultural identity of British cinema during these decades. Part 3 explores the channel's working relationships with film producers, and critically examines the role of Film on Four as a talent house for British filmmakers. Chapter 5 looks in detail at the channel's film-funding model, while Chapter 6 explores working relationships between Commissioning Editors and film companies via case studies of two British film companies that worked regularly with the channel in the 1980s and early 1990s: Working Title and Palace Pictures. Chapter 7 focuses in more closely on the channel's role in supporting and developing new filmmaking talent via the creation of short-film initiatives, and by examining the opportunities Film on Four provided to first-time directors. The distribution and exhibition of Films on Four in the USA and Europe is the subject of Part 4, which examines the importance of film festivals, international distribution deals and relationships with companies such as Miramax and PolyGram to the more corporate identity Channel 4 developed as a film producer from the mid-1990s.

In April 2022, the UK government announced its intention to privatise Channel 4, which has been publicly owned but commercially funded since its creation by Margaret Thatcher's Conservative government in the early 1980s. While in recent years this issue has become more pressing in an era of digital broadcasting and Video on Demand, public debates about whether Channel 4 should be privatised are nothing new: much like the BBC, the viability and sustainability of the channel's funding model have, for many decades, been a regular feature of public discourse about the role and function of Public Service Broadcasting in British cultural life. Since its inception Channel 4 has continually walked a fine line between its PSB remit to commission 'original' and 'innovative' content that caters to diverse audiences and its need to secure the revenue to fund its programming, which, unlike the BBC's programming, is funded solely by advertising. Often lost in these conversations, however, is any account of the industrial and cultural importance of Film4 to the UK's cultural and creative industries.

For almost forty years the channel has developed, produced and co-produced films that have been widely considered hallmarks of British national cinema, films which would never have been made if not for the economic protection the channel afforded. Nothing proves the rule quite like the exception: in 1998 the channel consolidated its film development, production and distribution activities under the banner of a new film studio, FilmFour, with the aim of investing in larger-scale filmmaking and competing with Hollywood companies. The channel's biggest box-office hit during these years was Damien O'Donnell's low-budget comedy *East is East*, which had in fact been commissioned under the wholly cultural remit of the previous Film on Four model. With the collapse of FilmFour in 2002 came the belated realisation that Channel 4 did not have the money or the infrastructure to compete with Hollywood, but it did have what every major film studio lacks: a cultural policy towards film that is determined by its public service remit. This has always been the inherent value of the channel's model of PSB broadcaster-funded film production: it allows for opportunities to fail, and therefore allows for opportunities to innovate.

Note

1. Here 'Film4' is used as a catch-all term to encompass the channel's various film financing and development initiatives, including Film on Four (1982–1998) and FilmFour (1998–2002).

Part 1

Film Policy

Chapter 1

Getting into film

Channel 4 made its memorable entrance onto the British broadcasting scene on 2 November 1982, but the pre-history of the channel stretches back almost two decades earlier. Intellectual and political pressure for a fourth channel had been building from the 1960s, and this was the subject of complex debates which had their roots in clashing political ideologies. What would a new channel look like? And would ITV or the BBC run it, or would it be independent? After the Pilkington Committee allocated the third channel to the BBC in 1962, there was an assumption that there would later be a fourth, and that this would essentially become ITV2. British broadcasting was dominated by the BBC and ITV, so for many it seemed natural that ITV would run the new channel, just as the BBC had BBC2. But this idea was unsatisfactory for those who felt that broadcasting was stifled by the two main broadcasters. A more truly independent outlet was needed.

The Labour government under Prime Minister Harold Wilson deferred the allocation of the fourth channel throughout the 1960s due to other commitments. In 1970, partly fuelled by a suspicion of commercial broadcasting, the Labour government decided that a committee of enquiry should be formed to debate the future of broadcasting. The committee was subsequently deferred by the incoming Conservative government but reconvened after Labour was re-elected in 1974, by which time feelings towards the fourth channel had changed. The committee, chaired by Lord Annan, published a report which set out the terms for the creation of the new channel.[1] The question of what was to be done with the 'fourth channel', which had spanned almost two decades, culminated in the 1977 Annan Report on the Future of Broadcasting.

For years programme makers had struggled to find an outlet for their ideas, with various pressure groups formed which aimed towards achieving greater public control of broadcasting production.[2] Anthony Smith, Director of the British Film Institute (1979–1988) and a key player in the campaign for the fourth channel, suggested the idea of a 'publishing house', where the new channel would not own studios or make programmes but would instead commission them from independent producers. Groups such as the Association of Independent Producers (AIP) and The Channel 4 Group campaigned for the rights and interests of independent producers. While the ideal outcome for producers would be for the new channel to be run under the auspices of an Open Broadcasting Authority (OBA), this met with financial and ideological obstacles. However, these groups did campaign successfully to keep the new channel from becoming ITV2. Ultimately, the channel would be regulated by the Independent Broadcasting Authority (IBA) and funded by a levy on ITV, who would in turn be responsible for the channel's advertising. Most importantly, it would provide an outlet for independent producers by committing to obtain half its programming from sources other than the ITV companies. These aspirations towards diversity in programming had been summarised succinctly in the Annan Report:

> Our society's culture is now multi-racial and pluralist: that is to say, people adhere to different views of the nature and purpose of life and expect their own view to be expressed in some form or other. The structure of broadcasting should reflect this variety.[3]

The report recommended the creation of a fourth channel that would be 'experimental in form and content', and indeed the concept of 'innovation' was subsequently written into the 1980 Broadcasting Act that created Channel 4. Similarly enshrined in its original remit was the idea that the channel would function as a mouthpiece for those in society whose experiences had previously been marginalised by the BBC and ITV. It was to operate as a 'publishing house', commissioning programming from the independent sector, which, following the channel's creation, emerged practically overnight. It would break the monopoly of broadcasting by providing an outlet for new voices and talents, while its creation gave birth to an independent sector which would thrive or fail according to the vagaries of the market.

The early years of Film on Four

Although the idea of the new fourth channel directly financing British film production wasn't directly addressed in the Annan Report, this had long been an ambition of the channel's first Chief Executive, Jeremy Isaacs. In a speech delivered at the Edinburgh Television Festival in 1979 (a speech which was widely seen as his unofficial application for the post), Isaacs stated his intention to 'make, or help make, films of feature length for television here, and for the cinema abroad'.[4] As he prepared to take up his position, Isaacs and the channel's new Commissioning Editor for Fiction, BBC Pebble Mill veteran David Rose, defined their idea for a new broadcasting strand called 'Film on Four'. The channel allocated around £6 million each year to commission feature films through its Drama Department (a move that would have far-reaching effects, particularly as, not to be outdone, the BBC followed suit with Screen 1 and Screen 2 in the late 1980s and later with BBC Films). The original aim was to commission around twenty low-budget films each year from independent producers, some of which would be fully funded, but most of which (for financial reasons) would be co-productions. The channel would be working with the film industry and co-producing British films on a regular basis: a move that was completely unprecedented in the history of British film and television. Film on Four soon diversified to include a number of international co-productions as well as partnerships with other UK broadcasters. In the early days of the channel's operation, the theatrical release of Films on Four in UK cinemas was a privilege granted to only a few select productions, but this soon became more common throughout the 1980s and increased considerably into the 1990s. 'Film on Four' was the name given to the films commissioned and financed by Channel 4 which had their premieres on UK television between 1982 and 1998, but this title is also used as a catch-all term for the channel's film production and development activities. Film on Four operated within the Fiction (later Drama) department of the channel, first under the aegis of David Rose (between 1982 and 1990) and then under David Aukin (between 1990 and 1998).

Channel 4's contribution as a film sponsor should be seen in the light of debates surrounding the occasionally antagonistic relationship between cinema and television in the decades prior to the channel's establishment, and it should be noted that these are discussions which were specifically British in character. In Britain, feature films had provided broadcasters with hours of cheap programming at a time when the film industry was in decline. Filmmakers argued that broadcasters should give something back, and that some measure of support should be directed from broadcasters to the film industry.[5] Elsewhere in Europe, however, film and television had already established a symbiotic relationship. Indeed, according to David Rose, West German broadcasting came to represent the real model for Film on Four policy.[6] Though the historical parallels and differences are undoubtedly complex, it is interesting to note that, in its early years, Film on Four encountered some of the same critical objections which characterised the co-dependence of film and television in West Germany. According to Martin Blaney, prejudiced accounts of the situation abounded, with many critics accusing television of being the source of the German film industry's ills, while the press tended to represent the relationship between film and television using analogies of squabbling siblings with television characterised as the 'upstart younger brother'.[7]

Of the fifteen to twenty films financed or co-financed by the channel each year, some were to be given theatrical releases before television transmission, and some were to be made directly for television. Pragmatically, theatrical release was not considered when Isaacs made his speech at the Edinburgh Festival in 1979, which was due partly to the Cinematograph Exhibitors' Association (CEA) rule that films could only be shown on television five years after first-run exhibition (reduced to three in 1980), and partly to the fact that union agreements meant that television films were simply cheaper to produce. In 1986, the CEA introduced measures to exclude films costing under £1.25m, an exclusion which would be automatic providing details of the films were sent to the Association in advance of broadcast. In 1988, this exclusion barrier was raised to £4m following a successful campaign led by the channel's Managing Director, Justin Dukes. This rapid acquiescence on the part of the CEA was indicative of the culture shift brought about by the channel in its first six years of operation.

Within a few years the channel had achieved theatrical and critical successes with productions like Stephen Frears's 1985 film *My Beautiful Laundrette* and Chris Bernard's *Letter to Brezhnev*, released in the same year. It had also entered into high-profile international co-productions with films like Wim Wenders' *Paris, Texas* (1984). At the Cannes Film Festival in 1987, Channel 4 gained public recognition of its successful film-funding practices when David Rose was awarded the prestigious Rossellini Award for Services to Cinema. The award signified a coming-of-age moment in the history of Film on Four, bringing with it international recognition of the channel's commitment to British film culture during bleak years for the domestic industry, and its increasing involvement in European co-productions.

Channel 4's film policy

In 1990, David Aukin succeeded Rose as Head of Drama at a time when Channel 4 was preparing to move into a more commercial broadcasting ecology under new Chief Executive Michael Grade. In

1993 the channel was to begin selling its own advertising, and was also facing a more competitive broadcasting market, post-deregulation, with the expansion of cable and satellite channels. This meant that the channel would continue to walk an increasingly fraught line between adhering to the remit to be innovative and original while still managing to attract advertisers in order to generate sufficient revenue to fund its programming. In the face of increased corporatisation, Aukin diversified the output of Film on Four, funding more populist films and targeting younger audiences while still supporting the types of low-budget British features that had long been the staple of the channel's film output. The following list, titled 'Channel 4's Policy toward Film', was written by David Aukin in 1996 and provides an accurate, if tongue-in-cheek, overview of the channel's ethos as a film financier:

1. To encourage predominantly British filmmakers to make films that will work both in cinemas and on television
2. To provide opportunities for filmmakers at the start of their careers
3. To commission the most talented filmmakers available
4. To commission films that would not be made without our finance
5. To commission films so that they can be made as intended by the filmmaker, with the proviso that we are not only Commissioners but also editors
6. To encourage filmmakers from all sections of society
7. To encourage films which can work within the industry but at the same time retain an individual voice and identity
8. To encourage the making of films from original screenplays dealing with contemporary themes rather than adaptations or the dreaded biopic
9. To only commission films where the Commissioning Editor is passionate about the material
10. To ignore all of the above except number 9.[8]

The list, while facetious in tone, takes a clear view regarding the differences between television and film (implying that while broadcasters have policies, film producers do not, a nod to the unusual position Channel 4's Drama Department occupied between these two industries). This list is also quite rare; it is difficult to find information about the channel's film policy written down in such a prescriptive way. Indeed, point 10 jokingly reinforces just how non-prescriptive the channel's policy towards film was by highlighting the fact that most of these points have been ignored at various stages of the life of Film on Four. Despite his flippant tone, Aukin's characterisation is a relatively accurate and useful overview of Film on Four policy at different times between 1982 and 1998, and as such his points are worth examining systematically.

Point 1 states that the channel should 'encourage predominantly British filmmakers to make films that will work both in cinemas and on television'. The idea that films could work both theatrically and on television was perhaps one of the trickiest aspects of the channel's approach to film, however, and one which has generated the most debate on an industrial as well as aesthetic level. Furthermore, throughout the 1980s and 1990s the channel also supported and co-funded a number of European productions, including Wim Wenders' *Paris, Texas* and Louis Malle's *Damage* (1996), sometimes to criticisms that it was not doing enough to support British directors. Channel 4 was involved in almost 300 productions from 1982–1998, providing opportunities to new filmmaking talent, resulting in greater variety in the output of the British film industry and to an extent sustaining the industry throughout the 1980s and early 1990s, when finance was particularly scarce. However, not everyone responded positively to Channel 4's involvement in film. The producer Don Boyd famously argued that Channel 4 taught British cinema to 'think small', to rely on predominantly low-budget and visually unambitious modes of filmmaking.[9]

In general, there are challenges in talking about productions made firstly for television broadcast, and secondly for theatrical exhibition. There is a whole body of academic scholarship relating to the aesthetic and technological similarities and differences between cinema and television, with much of this scholarship (notably work by John Hill and Martin McLoone [1996] and more recently Jason Jacobs and Stephen Peacock [2013]) concerned with the question of what exactly makes a film 'cinematic'.[10] David Rose has argued that many of the plays he produced at Pebble Mill in the 1970s were films but without the benefit of a theatrical release. These ideas will be unpacked in greater detail in Chapter 3, but it is worth noting here that definitions of the 'cinematic' have historically been intangible among industry professionals, critics and academics. For Film on Four Commissioning Editors it was also difficult to tell whether a film might work *both* in the cinema and on television. For example, Stephen Frears's *My Beautiful Laundrette* is an example of a film which was shot on 16mm and made for television but which did very well theatrically. As we shall see, whether a Film on Four secured theatrical release largely depended on the interest of distributors. Furthermore, the decision of whether to invite distributors to buy rested with the company which had majority rights in the production, which was not necessarily Channel 4.

Point 2 illustrates the channel's commitment to new talent, and indeed around half of the films commissioned by the channel between 1982 and 1998 provided opportunities to writers and directors making their feature-film debuts. However, the channel also consistently worked with many established filmmakers such as Ken Loach, Mike Leigh and Stephen Frears. Point 5 states that the films should be made as intended by the filmmaker, although David Aukin in particular could, on occasion, be editorially difficult. For example, in 1992 he famously refused to release the money for *The Crying Game* (Neil Jordan, 1992) until the script had been re-written to his satisfaction, which resulted in a grand total of seventeen redrafts.[11]

In point 8 Aukin writes about his disdain for the 'dreaded biopic', though *The Madness of King George* (Nicholas Hytner, 1994) was one of the most successful films he commissioned during his time at the channel. David Rose had also expressed a dislike for adaptations and Second World War dramas, but he nevertheless funded the E. M. Forster adaptations *A Room with a View* (James Ivory, 1985) and *Maurice* (James Ivory, 1987). Furthermore, Michael Radford's *Another Time, Another Place* (1983), which is both an adaptation *and* a Second World War drama, was one of the most successful early Films on Four, winning a BAFTA and an *Evening Standard* British Film Award in 1984.[12]

Point 9 illustrates that in terms of the types of films the channel funded, in many cases this was simply a matter of the personal taste of the Commissioning Editor – and while this was rarely prescriptive, CEs could be notoriously vague about their likes and dislikes. David Rose was difficult to pin down on exactly what he thought constituted a good Film on Four script, simply stipulating that submissions should be 'fresh' and 'unfamiliar, if possible'.[13] David Aukin was equally ambiguous, stating in an interview that 'I don't really know what a Channel 4 film is, except that when you see it, you know it'.[14] Point 10 reinforces the importance of personal taste by jokingly noting the prerogative of the Commissioning Editor to 'ignore all of the above'. This point in particular outlines a key issue that must be discussed when thinking about Film on Four's remit, its policy and the way in which it operated. It was Jeremy Isaacs and David Rose who originally determined the direction of Film on Four, strongly influenced by the German ZDF model and shaped by Channel 4's wider remit to encourage innovation in the form and content of its programming. But beyond this outline, the channel's film policy was neither restrictive nor dogmatic. According to David Rose, it was also rarely talked about within the department:

> There was no clear policy. I was simply asked to commission films that we felt would work in the cinema. They were films; they were for Channel 4 viewers. I have always based any judgement on the quality of writing and direction. We made them to cinema standards on 35mm.[15]

The process of film financing within the BBC was far more bureaucratic, and David Aukin's BBC counterpart Mark Shivas would have to defer to various committees before he could commit to a production.[16] To illustrate, in 1997 Scala producer Nik Powell stated that the channel 'delegated the decision making process to one person or a team of people with no interference from above', which made it 'much easier to deal with than its colleagues at the BBC'.[17] Similarly, Mike Leigh's *Secrets and Lies* (1996) was in development with the BBC for 15 months before a deal was finally put in place. After it began to look as though this deal might fall through, Aukin was able to commission the film for Channel 4 within a matter of days.[18] The creative autonomy of Rose and Aukin was, in many ways, protected. Although Film on Four under Aukin did indeed begin to function with an eye to commercial viability, the strand still benefitted from the security of guaranteed annual budgets and a strong drive towards cultural rather than economic imperatives. As Paul Webster noted, Film on Four under Rose and Aukin:

> was a creative model, not an economic model … It had the trappings of a business under David Aukin but nevertheless he didn't have to answer to any economic brief whatsoever … David basically refused to answer any question he was asked about the economic value of anything he did, because he argued that [he had a] solely creative brief, which was fantastic.[19]

Funding was not doled out according to checklists and committees, and although one can speculate about the fairness of such a system, the result was film finance that was more readily available to producers with fewer restrictive criteria than perhaps would be the case with film-funding bodies. It is also worth noting, however, that in some ways Film on Four did operate similarly to grant-funding bodes which allocate public subsidies for the arts, if only in the sense that projects were often funded according to their cultural merit, and the channel rarely expected to make significant profits from these productions.

Conclusion

Film on Four operated as part of Channel 4, as part of one programming department among many, but Rose and Aukin were also acting in some ways as film producers. In the selection of promising scripts for production, in having editorial input at the pre-production and post-production stages and in seeing films through to theatrical release, Aukin, Rose and their teams carried out many of the actions which would have been typical of a film studio. Unlike broadcasters, film companies tend not to have clearly defined policies because in the film industry, variety and adaptability are the key to success. Rose and Aukin enjoyed a large degree of autonomy, and it was not unusual for key creative decisions to be taken by one or two people. This autonomy is suggestive of recognition on the part of the channel that selecting potential films for production involves risk and demands flexibility, qualities that are dependent on personal taste, instinct, and the freedom to make decisions. Film on Four acted as both a film company and as part of a television programming department within a broadcaster which had a clear cultural remit with regard to supporting new talent and funding non-commercial productions, and this has been reflected in its policies and *modus operandi*.

Notes

1. Andrew Crisell, *An Introductory History of British Broadcasting*, 2nd edn (London: Routledge, 2005), 202.
2. *Ibid.*, 202.
3. House of Commons, 1976–1977, Home Office. *Report of the Committee on the Future of Broadcasting*, Cmnd. 6753-I, London, 30.
4. John Hill, *British Cinema in the 1980s: Issues and Themes* (Oxford: Clarendon Press, 1999), 54.
5. *Ibid.*, 54.
6. David Rose, interviewed by Justin Smith, 27 May 2010.
7. Martin Blaney, *Symbiosis or Confrontation? The Relationship Between the Film Industry and Television in the Federal Republic of Germany from 1950 to 1985* (Berlin: Edition Sigma, 1992).

8. David Aukin, 'Channel 4's Policy Toward Film', in *Big Picture, Small Screen: The Relations Between Film and Television*, ed. by John Hill and Martin McLoone (Luton: University of Luton Press, 1996), 183.

9. *British Television Drama in the 1980s*, ed. by George Brandt (Cambridge: Cambridge University Press, 1993), 14.

10. Jason Jacobs and Stephen Peacock, eds, *Television Aesthetics and Style* (London: Bloomsbury, 2013).

11. Anon., *Christian Science Monitor*, 26 March 1993.

12. Michael Coveney, *The World According to Mike Leigh* (London: Harper Collins, 1996), 185.

13. Hilary Brown, 'The Film Man', *Airwaves*, 13 (Winter, 1987/88).

14. Angus Finney, 'New Crew in Uncharted Waters', *Screen International*, 1 March 1991.

15. *Screen international*, 26 September 1997, 28–36.

16. *Ibid.*, 28–36.

17. *Ibid.*, 28–36.

18. *The Observer*, 23 June 1997.

19. Paul Webster, interviewed by Justin Smith and Laura Mayne, 23 April 2012.

Chapter 2

A matter of taste: Commissioning films

The creation of a Conservative government but ideologically left-leaning in its political origins, Channel 4 began broadcasting on 2 November 1982, arriving on British television screens in an explosion of spinning multicoloured rectangular blocks. The now familiar Channel 4 ident has undergone many changes over the years, but the essence of the design remains unchanged, and is in many ways symbolic of the channel's organisation and remit. Originally designed by Martin Lambie-Nairn, the ident consists of disparate blocks hanging in space, a fragmented, dynamic collection of moving parts that comes together to form a whole. From 1982 to the present day the ident has been suggestive of the idea of the channel pulling together creative forces into a discrete identity which is 'Channel 4'. The more modern idents are often embedded in spaces or landscapes, and the brand logo is often expressly linked to a particular region of the UK.

Setting up the channel: Charlotte Street, W1

If a broadcaster commissions the bulk of its programming from around the country, it follows that it does not necessarily matter where, geographically, that broadcaster is based. In reality, however, the physical location of Channel 4 mattered in 1982 and, judging by the media coverage generated by channel's move to Leeds in 2020, it continues to matter today. Dorothy Hobson, who enjoyed a considerable amount of access to the channel in its first few years of operation while working on her book *Channel 4: The Early Years and the Jeremy Isaacs Legacy*, writes about the choice of 60 Charlotte Street as the location of the channel's original headquarters:

> The building was located in the heart of London's W1 district, close to Wardour and Dean Street and other areas associated with

> the film and television industries. The London offices of most ITV companies and the Independent Television Companies Association (ITCA) building were not far away…One ITV executive told me that I could conduct the whole research for this book within a square mile around Charlotte Street. This may have been a slight exaggeration but it was not too far from the truth in that there is a concentration of power and influence and control within the television industry in this area.[1]

Hobson's book maintains an inspiring and optimistic tone throughout, but the way she narrates her account of Channel 4 in its earliest days provides an insight into a corporate culture that does not always depict the channel in the most flattering light. She describes an open-plan office space that was in many ways very trendy and ahead of its time, but devoid of the 'buzz' that might be expected of a television company. In her descriptions of the channel's daily operations she conjures a sense of Commissioning Editors wielding great power, of policies being driven by a few select people and a distinct lack of the kinds of management hierarchy or bureaucracy that characterised a broadcaster like the BBC – for better or, in some cases, worse.

John Ellis's account of working with the channel in 1983 is far less optimistic in tone. Ellis was among the first round of independents commissioned by Channel 4, and he describes the relationship between the channel and independent producers in the first year as akin to the relationship between an arts funder and a client, with some companies created on the basis of one commission. By the following year, Ellis writes that the relationship was one between freelancer and a more commercial institution, with some companies kept waiting and some contracts not renewed.[2] He describes Channel 4 as 'a rather odd bureaucracy, overstaffed in some areas, understaffed in others, and containing a number of conflicting ideologies and practices'. Ellis writes about the structural problems experienced by an independent sector that was disconnected from an organisation which commissioned its programmes centrally, and of the confusion on the part of independent producers regarding the planning and scheduling of their programmes in these early days.[3] It is difficult to imagine the chaos of a sector created overnight, whose existence was determined by one source of funding, with the organisational identity and processes of the 'commissioning house' or 'publisher broadcaster' constantly being negotiated and re-negotiated. The channel's Commissioning Editors were responsible for selecting which programmes to produce and were therefore the people on whom the new independent sector depended, and this was a vast responsibility to be centred in the hands of a select few.

What did a Commissioning Editor do?

The job of the Commissioning Editor was not just to approve scripts, but to work in a number of capacities. As Jeremy Isaacs set out in a programme policy document in 1985, these were governed by a number of areas – what we might think of as levels of 'influence'. Upper levels of 'influence' included: Channel 4's terms of reference with the IBA programme policy statement; the channel's overall programme policy, as developed by the board and the programme committee; the number of hours of programming allocated to a certain area (such as news, sport, etc), and the financial resources budgeted for that subject area.[4] The Commissioning Editor was directly responsible to the Chief Executive and/or the Programme Controller. David Rose was directly responsible to Jeremy Isaacs, for example, with no management structures in between, whereas in the early 1990s (after the channel had undergone internal changes under Isaacs' successor Michael Grade) David Aukin was initially responsible to Liz Forgan, and *then* to Michael Grade.

In 1985, Jeremy Isaacs outlined the role of the Commissioning Editor as follows:

> The CE must:
> - Agree general policy for the strands/programmes they are responsible for and communicate this to Programme controller
> - Also communicate this policy to programme suppliers and ITV companies
> - 'Where appropriate', initiate projects in line with this policy by approaching the production companies and inviting them to participate
> - Choose and distinguish among competing submissions from programme makers
> - Agree a detailed brief with the programme supplier
> - Liaise with the programme supplier during production – by visiting locations, viewing rushes etc – 'to ensure the programme is being produced in accordance with the editor's requirements'
> - Liaise with Programme Cost Controllers for all of the above
> - Liaise with programme controller and the Head of Programme Planning to discuss appropriate scheduling of programmes
> - Liaise with press dept to discuss the best way for the programme to be publicised

- Ensure that the admin details associated with programme transmission (music, billings, cue sheets, presentation details etc) are dealt with
- Discussions with the Chief Executive, the programme controller and discussions in the Programme Planning Committee and Programme review committee helps to 'determine the editorial direction of the channel'
- The CE must represent the channel to independent producers, at conferences, at festivals etc.[5]

A Commissioning Editor had a wide range of responsibilities, many of which involved negotiation with various departments to agree budgets/slot/publicity for a programme, but also to monitor the programme to make sure that it was falling within the requirements agreed between the producer and the channel. The Commissioning Editor also had editorial input where programme policy was concerned, through discussion with upper management.

There is little evidence to suggest that Film on Four was approached with any defined and detailed commissioning strategy, either in 1982 or when David Aukin took over as Head of Drama in 1990. In the case of Film on Four (as with other departments) it was possible for anyone to submit a script or treatment, which could be submitted independently or through an already established production company. From 1982, David Rose and his department regularly received around 2,000 scripts and treatments per year, while David Aukin regularly received between 60–100 scripts per week.[6] These would then be condensed into synopses by a team of readers, with likely submissions to be discussed by Senior Commissioning Editors at fortnightly meetings.[7] If all of this sounds complex, the channel's structure in its early years was actually fairly simple in terms of managerial hierarchy. As Hobson writes:

> The first floor was the heart of the channel and the editors had their own area where their offices were clustered. Tiny and glass walled partitions meant that the editors and their visitors were visible to everyone passing by … Secretaries were located near by [sic] and everyone was within a few yards of Jeremy's office. They could walk in to question him, rail at some decisions, or just to seek advice. And they did.[8]

However, as broadcast hours increased and the editorial team grew, this became increasingly unfeasible. Michael Grade's arrival in 1988 saw some internal restructuring, and further reorganisation when the channel moved towards selling its own advertising in 1993, with an obvious growth in advertising and sales departments.[9]

Throughout these changes, Film on Four remained largely autonomous within the Drama Department and the wider structure of the channel. For example, while many commissioned scripts would have been reviewed by Jeremy Isaacs, the Chief Executive normally avoided direct interference, even where he did not agree with particular aspects of the commission.[10] According to Isaacs, it was a 'hands-off' relationship that worked very well. Discussing Rose's achievements in 2004, he wrote:

> It is not just what David did that is instructive, but how he did it: no committees of consultants; no focus groups or market-testing. Just an eye for a situation, a nose for a script, and a mind of his own to make the critical judgement.[11]

David Aukin enjoyed a similar level of autonomy, stating in an interview in 1995:

> what I commission is a reflection of my own personal taste and judgement; it would be difficult having to defer to committees. There is a very simple chain of command: I am responsible to John Willis (Director of Programming) and then Michael Grade.[12]

Grade also stated that he had never read a Film on Four script, preferring to allow Aukin a '*totally* free rein'.[13]

Plays for television? David Rose (1982–1990)

David Rose was responsible for Fiction (and later 'Drama') but he did have increasing help in the form of script editor Walter Donohue and playwright David Benedictus.[14] After Benedictus left, Peter Ansorge joined the team, as well as Assistant Commissioning Editor Karin Bamborough, who had previously worked in the Arts department of the channel under Michael Kustow. Bamborough often dealt with issues arising from *Brookside*, although she also commissioned the playwright Hanif Kureishi to write *My Beautiful Laundrette* for the channel, and stepped in to save Chris Bernard's *Letter to Brezhnev* from financial ruin in 1984.[15] The drama 'team' remained small throughout the life of Film on Four. For example, when David Aukin joined the channel he worked with Colin Leventhal and Sarah Geater, who dealt with legal and financial issues and cost accounting, leaving Aukin relatively free to focus on commissioning the work.[16] Aukin also hired help in the form of American script editor Jack Lechner (who helped with the troubled script editing and pre-production of Neil Jordan's *The Crying Game* in 1991). Lechner was succeeded by Assistant Commissioning Editor Allon Reich, who, among other things, was responsible for the Drama Department's short-film strand Short and Curlies.[17]

Films on Four, particularly in the early 1980s, were often seen as having strong links to single plays, many of which were shot on film in locations around Britain. In 1982, before plans for the theatrical release of Film on Four productions had been fully developed, Jeremy Isaacs even referred to them as such in a publication for Channel 4 viewers:

> *Film on Four*, at 9pm on Wednesdays, is a series of single plays filmed for television – and we're very proud of them. After *First Love*, *Remembrance* and *Praying Mantis* you'll realise that each is very different and that each is a real television event.[18]

Isaacs' view was not unusual; in newspapers and trade publications around this time, there was often a stylistic link made between early Films on Four and single plays. However, less commonly noted was the cross-fertilisation of talent and working practices between the BBC and Channel 4 with regard to these early films. As Head of Regional Drama at BBC Pebble Mill (1970–1981), David Rose had produced many of the most innovative plays of the decade before he moved to Channel 4 to become Head of Fiction, and his influence on the development of Film on Four was in part determined by his previous career. At Pebble Mill Rose was given a specific brief to commission work by regional writers and to raise the profile of the regions on mainstream television. The 1950s and 1960s had seen notable productions from the Birmingham Drama Department, but from 1970 it was to gain complete autonomy from London for the first time.[19] Rose's role as producer at Pebble Mill was thus unusual, in that it enabled him to work outside many of the constraints faced by other BBC producers.

Writers were eager to work at Pebble Mill because they felt it was a space which offered creative opportunities. For example, David Mercer was able to make a 30-minute play called *You, Me and Him* (1973) where the id, ego and superego were all played by one actor. This production was expensive and involved over 300 manual video edits after every shot.[20] Rose also encouraged David Hare, the playwright and theatre director, to direct as well as write *Licking Hitler* (1978), which is often critically appraised as being one of the most stylistically notable examples of the single play.[21] Some of the work produced at Pebble Mill was experimental; David Rudkin's *Penda's Fen* (1974) was a surprising departure from the strong vein of naturalism which was often seen to dominate the single play. If *My Beautiful Laundrette* has often been described as the 'archetypal Film on Four', David Hare says that *Penda's Fen* embodied the 'culture' that Rose fostered at Pebble Mill in the 1970s:

> When I saw Penda's Fen, I just couldn't believe it. And that is the whole BBC Birmingham culture right there, which was David Rose letting people do what they wanted and nobody in London knowing what was going on. You know: 'The earth splits open? Oh yeah?' There's just no way a London producer and script editor would have been having that. But my God, that film went out at nine-thirty at night on a majority channel, it's incredible … And how bold to do it![22]

At Channel 4, Rose's role as a Commissioning Editor was in many ways similar to the position he had occupied at the BBC. Indeed, he stated that the move to Channel 4 was 'a smooth transition. It seemed to me [that] it was pretty well exactly what I was doing in Pebble Mill'.[23] Script editor Peter Ansorge, who had worked with Rose at Pebble Mill, also echoed this view, stating that

> I did not find the way David worked at Film on Four any different to the way in which he worked at Pebble Mill. He gave the producers freedom, autonomy, but he was always there with what he thought about scripts, in the cutting room he was exactly the same.[24]

One reason for this 'smooth transition' perhaps existed at the level of creative independence. Isaacs had liked what he had seen coming out of Pebble Mill, and trusted Rose to continue this work at Channel 4 in selecting variety and innovation and in supporting new talent. In stylistic terms, the move was not only a transition for Rose, but, perhaps, a natural progression. At Pebble Mill, Rose had already shown a preference for working with film, and at Channel 4 he would be working almost exclusively in this medium. Moreover, he saw the idea of films for television as the natural outcome of the single play, stating in an interview that many BBC plays 'could well, I think have had a release in the cinema'.[25] Indeed, in 2011 *Penda's Fen* came in at number 76 in a *Time Out* poll of the top 100 Best British films, suggesting its retrospective status as 'film' rather than 'play', at least among the 150 industry professionals involved in the survey.[26]

Critics at the time noted that many Films on Four displayed an acute sense of geography, which, as James Saynor argued, followed a 'formula of socially displaced characters firmly positioned within a regional landscape'; a formula which had 'also characterised the offerings of Rose's writers in the 70s'.[27] Indeed, many of these films can trace their influences to plays by Alan Plater, Ken Loach/Tony Garnett and Mike Leigh, while Rose also continued to work with these writers and directors at Channel 4. These productions aimed at capturing the identity of regional communities, exploring the relationship between character and landscape and examining the ways in which 'place' can shape individual identity. Indeed, just about the only process for selecting scripts that Rose would admit to in early interviews was that they should 'take strength from a sense of the particular, a sense of time and place'.[28] The link between Pebble Mill and early Films on Four may seem a tenuous one, especially considering that over two-thirds of these early films do not fit into this particular mode. But with Rose's emphasis on the regional, his preference for film, and his own methods of working (providing a base of talent, offering creative freedom, acting as a benevolent patron but offering advice and encouragement when needed) his previous career as Head of English Regions Drama does need to be considered as being extremely influential to the output of Film on Four in the first few years of the channel's operation.

Film on Four goes to the movies: David Aukin (1990–1998)

David Aukin took over as Head of Drama in 1990, following his time as Chief Executive of the National Theatre. At first, he was very much an unknown quantity to filmmakers, having had no previous experience of film production. However, finding and encouraging new talent was equally as important to Aukin as it had been to David Rose, and he was also anxious that Film on Four should continue to take risks, even though the channel was facing the move towards selling its own advertising in 1993. Aukin was also concerned with having a higher degree of editorial control, in funding fewer films while investing more equity in each, thus having more of a say in the direction of the production. However, while

Aukin's influence on policy is easily identifiable, thematic continuities across the films he commissioned are harder to recognise, perhaps because his commissions really broadened the range of films that the channel sponsored. Whereas with many of the Films on Four of the 1980s we can identify a very contemporary, social-realist aesthetic, after 1990 we can note a very definite change in direction. Indeed, Aukin has cited one film in particular as providing the catalyst for that change. In 1991, the channel entered into a co-production with Palace Pictures on the Richard Stanley film *Dust Devil*, a supernatural horror fantasy set in Namibia about a demonic creature that poses as a hitchhiker and preys on lonely drifters. Though the production background of this film will be examined in more detail later in this book, it is worth noting here that the commission was a conscious decision on the part of Aukin to sever the last link with BBC single plays and herald a move away from the types of production that Film on Four had been perceived as making in the past: visually unambitious, social-realist films. For Aukin, the channel made 'feature films', and he argued that the idea of making a film and *then* deciding to put it in the cinema was the wrong approach.[29] Throughout the 1980s, around 60% of Films on Four had gained theatrical exposure.[30] Under Aukin, this moved closer to 90%.

Aukin was often accused by critics of taking Film on Four in a more commercial direction. He tended to be interested in the more visually thrilling, and did not shy away from commissioning genre films like *Dust Devil* or *Shallow Grave* (Danny Boyle, 1994). However, to say that this is what Film on Four became would be misleading. Aukin's tenure was characterised by variety. He would take greater equity stakes in larger-budget productions like Louis Malle's *Damage*, but continued to fully fund uncommercial films like Ken Loach's *Riff-Raff* (1991) for modest amounts, even though, as he stated, 'the sales people loathed the fact that I kept supporting Ken Loach, [but] I felt it was part of my job to maintain the support for these proven directors'.[31] He also invested in small-scale international co-productions like Allison Anders' *Mi Vida Loca* (1993) and continued to fund more experimental films like Terence Davies' *The Neon Bible* (1995).

Like Rose, Aukin was considerably influenced by his previous career, and sought to marry the artistic and the innovative with popular appeal. He stated:

> I've spent my time in the theatre trying to make quality work popular and accessible to as wide a public as possible. I never took

pride in producing wonderful work and then nobody turning up. Try doing good work people also want to see. That's the challenge.[32]

Aukin increasingly adopted the rhetoric of a film studio, referring to Film on Four's yearly 'slate' and 'strike rate', and ran Film on Four much in the way of a film company, commissioning a wide variety of films while realising that in terms of theatrical release (where the channel had equity stakes), two-thirds of those films might flop, a couple might break even and one or two might be very successful. In this era, the relationship between commercial and cultural imperatives became more complex. Low-budget filmmaking remained a firm part of Film on Four even though many productions were increasingly viewed with more of an eye to audience reception and theatrical distribution.

Aukin and Rose were not film producers in the traditional sense, although the policy of seeing films through from script to distribution stage meant that they enjoyed an almost paternalistic role more closely associated with a studio executive than a television producer. Indeed, the job of Rose and Aukin was to provide a space where writers and filmmakers could flourish, and to be confident in exercising taste and judgement in selecting scripts and backing productions. Aukin was headhunted for his role as Head of Drama by Senior Commissioning Editor Liz Forgan. According to Aukin, the channel did not hire a Commissioning Editor with hands-on filmmaking experience because, as she stated, 'your job isn't to make the films; it's to choose the people and the projects'.[33]

In a recent interview, producer Stephen Woolley noted the difference between working with David Rose and David Aukin:

> David Rose … was acting like a patron of the arts. Someone who would be giving money to, to … here you are, Peter Greenaway, here's your 100 grand, or 200 grand, or your 400 grand, and who's your producer? … Whereas I think David Aukin recognised that the distasteful world out there is the same world. We live in that world. There's not much we can do about it. And if you want to see good movies being made, if you want to see *Trainspotting* being made and properly released in America … you're going to have to embrace some of those distasteful people.[34]

Aukin was more willing than Rose to engage with commercial details. He was also known to work against the objectives of filmmakers and producers in the interests of the quality of a production. For example, in 1991 he fought a sustained campaign against Neil Jordan's script for

The Crying Game, refusing to release the £800,000 that the channel was investing until Jordan had redrafted the script to his satisfaction.[35] Aukin also encouraged Richard Curtis to make revisions to his script for *Four Weddings and a Funeral* (Mike Newell, 1994) because he felt that the characters were not developed sufficiently. He also stipulated that the film could not shoot until the Spring of that year as 'this was not a Winter film', which infuriated PolyGram, the other company backing the production.[36]

Channel 4 launches a film studio: Paul Webster (1998–2002)

'There is no pattern to the low budget British breakout picture in the last fifteen years – it's just luck.' – Paul Webster

Over the years Channel 4 has been a co-producer of films and these interests have taken the form of a series of broadcast strands, a channel and a standalone film studio. Film on Four has been considered as both separate from and connected to Channel 4, a distinct initiative and yet an integral part of the channel's history and identity. The decision to make FilmFour a standalone studio in 1998 was part of a process of professionalisation that had been gaining pace throughout the 1990s, and it was an integral aspect of Channel 4's new strategic direction under Chief Executive Michael Jackson from 1998.

Paul Webster took over from David Aukin as Head of the newly created standalone company FilmFour in 1998 and oversaw the venture until its collapse in 2002. In a 2012 interview, he reflected on his thoughts at the time about the consequences, both positive and negative, of FilmFour becoming more connected to the film industry and evolving a more distinctive brand identity outside of television broadcasting structures. Until 1998 Film on Four operated as part of the Drama Department but when Webster joined the channel, he emphasised the logic for having a separate office as well as a distinctive organisational identity:

And then we sort of streamlined the company a bit and then said, well actually if we're going to be a company, if we're going to be Film Four Limited, then we need to be together. So the next step was to say well we need either you put us all in one space at Horseferry Road, or, because we were all over the building, I couldn't find, it took me months to find the international distribution.[37]

The new premises of FilmFour were located near Channel 4's original headquarters on Charlotte Street, in the heart of Soho. This meant that for the first time FilmFour was, in the words of Paul Webster, 'literally, physically, a vertically integrated company'. FilmFour was no longer tied to the channel geographically, and in terms of policy the company was to proceed in an entirely different direction from its aims under Webster's predecessors. However, the venture did not pan out according to the ambitious vision of Channel 4's Chief Executive Michael Jackson. Webster's successor Tessa Ross speculates that the reasons for FilmFour's failure lay in the disconnect between the channel's aims and the finite amount of time, money and resources available:

> The first thing was that the pressure on FilmFour Ltd was so huge because it was all about delivering cash, and secondly it was impossible for them to do that in such a short space of time. If you asked, 'were there some good films at that time?', you'd say, 'Yes'. They made *Sexy Beast* (2000), *The Warrior* (2001), *The Motorcycle Diaries* (2004) to name a few – all great films. But their starting point was, 'We're going to have some hits'. And that was bloody difficult.[38]

Expectations were simply too high, and this was further complicated by the fact that FilmFour had grown to encompass marketing and distribution interests alongside production.

From the context of Webster's account, the real issues lay with the economic model FilmFour had adopted when he took over the strand in 1998. FilmFour was now housed in a separate building, but while the space was better able to be managed and controlled, and while lines of communication and professional relationships were more apparent, ultimately FilmFour ended up with less control over the films it financed. The films the company became involved with were bigger than Film on Four would have ordinarily been able to afford (part of a 'kill the middle' strategy on the part of Michael Jackson to fund big-budget films which might have a greater chance of becoming Hollywood hits). FilmFour's brief was now entirely commercial, and its only remit was to generate profit by funding box-office hits. Previously, although Film on Four had become more professional and developed international and distribution arms in the 1990s, Aukin's brief remained entirely about funding films with artistic, cultural and social relevance. This is not to say that FilmFour under Webster did not consider cultural value as a part of its priorities, or that the films funded in this era were solely commercial vehicles. However, working with the film industry on a larger scale meant that FilmFour was often a minority financier by necessity, and being a minority financier often meant being the last to have creative input and being the last party to get paid. According to Webster, if the company had continued to be housed at Channel 4's premises in Horseferry Road, FilmFour might 'have continued to export films that we could control'. But this was less about the organisational culture and dynamics, and more about maintaining creative and financial control over low-budget independent films where FilmFour could actually afford to invest larger amounts of equity. Following the collapse of the company, FilmFour became Film4, scaled down its film production and distribution operations and went back to Horseferry Road, and back to a policy of funding low-budget British films on principles of cultural and artistic merit rather than projected box-office returns.

Back to Basics: Tessa Ross (2002–2014)

Tessa Ross joined Channel 4 as Head of Drama in 2000 and controller of Film and Drama from 2002–2014. She had previously worked at the BBC from 1993–2000 running the Independent Commissioning Group for Drama. Ross's first concern was to re-establish the relationship between Film4 and the channel, while also continuing to nurture its relationships with the film industry. The new aim, according to Ross, was to make films that the channel wanted to show, while at the same time encouraging filmmakers and the film industry to work with Film4.[39] FilmFour had lost sight of its broadcasting origins, and Ross was more cognisant of the channel and how the films would work on television not in terms of aesthetic preoccupations but in terms of Channel 4's brand, market position and identity (as well as those of the Film4 Freeview channel). The new, scaled-back Film4 also had limited resources, so development was key to growing new projects and retaining control over the films the channel financed. Interviewed in 2012, Ross said that just under 20% of Film4's budget was invested in development, and this involved working with filmmakers and seeking out projects, not waiting for scripts to arrive.

The advent of National Lottery funding and the growth of BBC Films meant that the channel was no longer one of the few sources of funding for independent filmmakers. This was a more complex, competitive environment in which Film4 had to work to compete for talent and projects. Ross says of the pressures faced by her predecessor David Rose in the 1980s compared with the new competitive environment of the early 2000s:

> David Rose was the most wonderful Head of Film Four and is an example of how goodness and humanity can make talent grow … But at the time no-one else was doing it in that way. Now we're competing as well as building, so we've got to do a bit of what David was doing – as well as we can, because none of us can be David – but equally we've got to grow, and we've got to deal with America a hell of a lot more, we've got to deal with other money a hell of a lot more; we've got massive commercial pressures on us. It requires a little bit of a different process.[40]

The distinctive brand identity of Film4 was consolidated in the 2000s as a producer of films for television, but the guiding light, for Ross and her team, was cinema. What made Film4 different from BBC Films was that it was always filmmaker-driven, though Ross is keen to emphasise that this 'doesn't mean to say that the BBC doesn't make great work – it does. But it's very driven by the story and by its accessibility to the audience on television.'[41] She notes being congratulated on *We Need to Talk about Kevin* (2011) and *Fish Tank* (2009) (both funded by BBC Films) as an example of this – these are films that are often erroneously attributed to Channel 4 because they seem to fit well with the channel's brand identity, but also, according to Ross, because those films are 'about filmmaking'.

Conclusion

Channel 4's corporate organisation and, in particular, its status as a 'publishing house' are key to understanding its place in British broadcasting and its distinctive identity as a Public Service Broadcaster tasked with a remit to provide 'original' and 'innovative' programming content. Accounts of the channel's earliest days are characterised by a sense of haphazard egalitarianism, but this moved gradually towards a consolidation of managerial hierarchies and decision-making processes. It is possible that the fanfare which accompanied the channel's arrival gave way to a sense of punctured idealism for many independent producers whose high hopes for this agile new broadcaster were soon tempered by the pragmatic realities of the channel's commissioning structures. Nevertheless, a detailed examination of the channel's Drama/Film department reveals the extent to which creative decision-making would remain relatively unencumbered throughout the 1980s and 1990s (as opposed to, for example, the more complicated organisational structures of the BBC). The narrative of Film on Four/FilmFour/Film4 can be most usefully organised into discrete historical periods not by decade or by brand identity but by the tenure of each Commissioning Editor, such was the influence of the CE on the policy and direction of the channel's film financing activities.

Notes

1. Dorothy Hobson, *Channel 4: The Early Years and the Jeremy Isaacs Legacy* (London: I B. Tauris, 2007), 18.
2. John Ellis, 'Channel 4: Working Notes', *Screen*, 24:6 (1983), 37–51.
3. *Ibid.*, 39.
4. BFI Special Collections, Papers of Roger Graef, CF Paper 313, 'Commissioning Editors' work loads' (1985).
5. *Ibid.*
6. *Daily Telegraph*, 2 May 1995.
7. *Time Out*, 27 November 1983.
8. Hobson, *Channel 4: The Early Years*, 56.
9. Michael Kustow, 'Fight for 4's Future', *Broadcast*, 15 December 1989.
10. Peter Ansorge, interviewed by the Channel 4 and British Film Culture AHRC project team, 7 June 2011.
11. Jeremy Isaacs, 'Happy Birthday to the Leader with the Golden Touch'. Available at: <http://www.independent.co.uk/news/media/happy-birthday-to-the-leader-with-the-golden-touch-532406.html> (accessed 22 March 2011).
12. *Daily Telegraph*, 24 May 1995.
13. *Ibid.*
14. Paul Bonner with Leslie Aston, *Independent Television in Britain Volume 6: New Developments in Independent Television* (Basingstoke: Palgrave, 2003), 193.
15. *Ibid.*, 193.
16. David Aukin, interviewed by Justin Smith and Laura Mayne, 23 February 2012.
17. *Ibid.*
18. Jeremy Isaacs, 'Letter from the Chief Executive', *4 This Month* (November 1982).
19. Barry Hanson, 'The 1970s: Regional Variations', in *British Television Drama: Past, Present and Future*, ed. by Jonathan Bignell et al. (Basingstoke: Palgrave, 2000), 166–71, 60.
20. *Ibid.*, 61.
21. John Caughie, *Television Drama: Realism, Modernism, and British Culture* (Oxford: Oxford University Press, 2000), 180.
22. Lez Cooke, *British Television Drama* (London: BFI Publishing, 2003), 119.
23. David Rose, interviewed by Justin Smith, 7 May 2010.

24. Ansorge, 7 June 2011.
25. Hilary Brown, 'The Film Man', *Airwaves*, 13 (Winter, 1987/88).
26. Anon., '100 Best British Films' *Timeout*. Available at: <http://www.timeout.com/london/film/time-outs-100-best-british-films> (accessed 4 October 2013).
27. James Saynor, 'Writers' Television', *Sight and Sound*, 2:7 (November 1992), 30.
28. *Ibid.*
29. *Ibid.*
30. *Screen International*, 2 November 1992.
31. Aukin, 23 February 2012.
32. Anon., 'C4 pledges an extra 4m for feature film investment', *Screen International*, 5 May 1995.
33. Aukin, 23 February 2012
34. Stephen Woolley, interviewed by Justin Smith and Laura Mayne, 22 March 2012.
35. *Christian Science Monitor*, 26 March 1993.
36. Aukin, 23 February 2012.
37. Paul Webster, interviewed by Justin Smith and Laura Mayne, 23 April 2012.
38. Tessa Ross, interviewed by Justin Smith and Laura Mayne, 1 August 2013.
39. *Ibid.*
40. *Ibid.*
41. *Ibid.*

Part Two

Films on Four

Chapter 3

Can television be cinema?

It seems anachronistic, in an era when films are streamed on tablets, laptops, mobile phones and other personal devices, to talk about the essential differences between cinema and television, but this was a debate which preoccupied filmmakers, academics and critics as a direct result of Channel 4's unprecedented involvement in British cinema. If a film is made for television, and broadcast on television, then can we really call it a film? By that logic, shouldn't the television 'plays' of the 1970s also be classed as films? (As we have seen, *Penda's Fen*, originally a play for television, occasionally appears on 'best film' lists as one of the top British films of all time). Neil Jordan's *Angel* (1982), one of the channel's earliest film commissions and thus made at a time when the channel was not considering theatrical release for films screened in the Film on Four strand, complicates notions of what defines 'film' and 'television'. *Angel* is a haunting film about a man on a mission of vengeance, a visually and aurally poetic exploration of universal themes of life and death set amid sublime, sweeping Irish landscapes. *Angel* seems to exemplify what BFI head Mammoun Hassan, writing in the Spring 1984 edition of *Sight and Sound*, called the characteristically defining nature of cinema, which deals with the 'ineffable . . . that which cannot be expressed'. *Angel* was broadcast on Film on Four but has rarely if ever been considered a television drama.

To trace the history of *Angel* from its commission to its premiere on Channel 4 we must journey from high-minded ideas about the ineffability of cinema to the back streets of Cannes, where producer Stephen Woolley saw the film and decided to acquire it for Palace Pictures:

> I flew to London the next day and met with John Boorman who was the executive producer of it. And I said 'Look, I really would like . . . I'm starting this company, I only have one film, *Diva*, and a little horror film called *The Evil Dead* but if you could, I really want to show this [as] part of our company'. And he said, 'We can't because Channel 4 are going to broadcast it.' So I went back in to Channel 4, this time to another guy there – not Jeremy Isaacs, but the legal guys. I said look, I want to release it as a film, because I think if you put it on telly, it's more than that.[1]

Woolley asked Channel 4 to delay the film's transmission by three months so it could first have a limited theatrical screening and collect reviews. This, Woolley notes, is what characterised *Angel* as a 'film' rather than as a television play and cemented Neil Jordan's reputation as a film director. Understanding the complexities involved in acquiring a film for distribution in cinemas and eventual broadcast involves teasing out the legal nuances of theatrical exhibition and broadcast policy as well as the more philosophical issues thrown up by Channel 4's decision to finance 'films' as distinct from television drama.

Theatrical release

Prior to the arrival of Channel 4, few television companies were directly involved in film production. There were some exceptions to this; for example, Peter Hall's *Akenfield* was co-financed by LWT and given a limited cinema release in 1975.[2] Yet it remains the case that in 1980, few films were produced with television funding. By 1989, broadcasters were investing in 49% of British film productions.[3] While in the USA many film companies had historically cultivated television production interests, in Britain cinema and television had developed separately and companies tended not to collaborate for reasons of historical rivalry. The idea that television should support British film production had its genesis in the 1970s. In 1973, the Cinematograph Films Council had argued that a levy should be placed on films shown on television to support the ailing industry. The Terry Report of 1976 also recommended that producers seek better prices for their films from television, and proposed that a levy be placed on the yearly profits of the independent television companies.[4] But it was through the recommendations for the fourth channel detailed in the Annan Report that a partnership between film and television really came to fruition.

Releasing films in the cinema was not initially the intended goal for Films on Four. As David Rose stated:

> No one was discussing theatrical windows of any kind when the early films were commissioned, but of course *Remembrance* and *Angel* were all made six, if not nine, months ahead of our going on air, so the filmmakers naturally began to look for these opportunities and we welcomed that.[5]

The motivation for seeking out theatrical distribution was certainly not commercial, as domestic releases of Films on Four were unlikely to make significant returns for the channel and were likely to cost more to make than the average television drama. Indeed, in 1993, the channel admitted to the Monopolies and Mergers Commission that in ten years, only a handful of Films on Four had actually made a profit.[6] However, theatrical release did enable the channel to capitalise on critical attention and the prestige of the premiere. Film investment was also important for raising the international profile of the channel in a way that television drama could not. By January 1993, the channel had aired 152 films in the Film on Four slot, more than 60% of which had had theatrical exposure. More than 70% of these productions had also been entered into film festivals around the world.[7] And, though these films made very little money, a handful served to boost the channel's reputation, such as *My Beautiful Laundrette, Mona Lisa* (Neil Jordan, 1986) and *Wish You Were Here* (David Leland, 1987).[8]

Funding films for cinema release could also be extremely problematic, and could provoke tensions between the channel and filmmakers. For example, in 1984 Derek Jarman's *Caravaggio* was halted because the co-investors wanted to push for a three-year holdback on the film in order to maximise its theatrical potential. The issue for filmmakers and exhibitors was that films needed to have a decent theatrical run before premiering on television. But this created a problem, as it meant the channel would have to wait years to broadcast a film in which it had invested heavily. Furthermore, if a number of people had already seen the film in cinemas this could even be detrimental to television ratings. Curtailing a theatrical run could also hit small independent cinemas the hardest, particularly at a time when cinemagoing was in decline. Producer Simon Perry stated in an interview regarding the release of Mike Radford's *Another Time, Another Place*:

> The problem in Britain, basically, is that the release pattern is determined by Channel 4's involvement. We have on the table firm interest for theatrical release and the offer for a video release, but both are predicated on a one-year holdback.[9]

In some cases, the channel would try to hold back a film from transmission so that it could enjoy a longer theatrical run. The broadcast of Jerzy Skomilowski's *Moonlighting* (1982) was, like *Angel*, delayed so that the film could benefit from a theatrical window.[10] Schedules could also be arranged in order to pad out the time between Film on Four premiere seasons. Scheduling seasons of the broadcast strand Film on Four International (overseas films to which the channel had pre-bought television rights) in the gap between Film on Four seasons, the channel could allow a greater theatrical window to their domestic collaborators.[11]

Though holdbacks on some films were negotiated, the channel also faced significant problems with the Cinematograph Exhibitors' Association (CEA). Independent distributors had no rules regarding the maximum time for theatrical exposure, but larger distributors tended to operate under the CEA, which operated a three-year holdback.[12] For example, though *She'll Be Wearing Pink Pyjamas* (John Goldschmidt, 1985) received much interest from Rank and EMI, working with these exhibitors would delay broadcast by three years. The film's producer, Adrian Hughes, summed up the problem:

> We are concerned that C4 gives *Pyjamas* a proper theatrical release. At the same time, why should C4 pay for and commission a really good piece of filmed drama and yet by the time it comes on the box everybody has seen it?[13]

The option for the channel in this instance was to allow the run to go ahead but appeal against the holdback when its theatrical life was seen to be diminishing.[14]

In some cases, a three-year television holdback and a two-year cable holdback was necessary for commercial as well as cultural reasons, as this would allow a film to build up publicity as well as being able to exploit each market in turn. However, in the 1980s Channel 4 films tended to be released on independent circuits and in West End cinemas, and a film given a limited release would exhaust its theatrical life fairly quickly. In the case of films like *My Beautiful Laundrette, Letter to Brezhnev* and *Wetherby* (David Hare, 1985), though the theatrical life of these films had been exhausted within a few months, the channel was still obliged to wait three years before screening them on television.[15] According to the British Screen Advisory Council, 'For a television company, investing in British cinema productions (with outstanding critical success) this was of considerable embarrassment and threatened the collapse of the Film on Four series.'[16] Paul Webster, Head of FilmFour between 1998 and 2002, reflected on the issues this caused:

> The more successful a film becomes, the more you're using up the potential TV audience. Then the more you exploit it in other mediums, like cinema, video at the time, DVD, the more you are pushing back the transmission date, so ironically the films that Film4 were making by the time I was there were of little value to the channel itself. The

channel needed premieres and by their very nature, the theatrical films we were making couldn't fulfil that need.[17]

In 1986 the CEA introduced an exemption from this three-year rule for films with budgets under £1.25m, although the channel's problems in this area would not be ironed out until later, when the CEA's exemption threshold was raised to £4m in 1988. The issues facing Channel 4 in funding Films on Four for theatrical release were not solely practical. The decision to invest in the British film industry also generated much debate regarding the aesthetic consequences of the involvement of a broadcaster in film production – debates which the following section will explore in greater detail.

'Too slight for cinema, too slack for television'?

In many ways, television and cinema had converged decades prior to the arrival of Channel 4. For example, in the late 1950s, the advent of videotape technology meant that television dramas could be recorded, rather than shot live, which opened up greater possibilities for the medium. Television was also an avid consumer of cinema product, and film began to make up a significant percentage of television schedules, not to mention the fact that, in time, television screens gradually began to get bigger, and cinema screens smaller.[18] There was some cross-over of personnel (writers, directors and actors) between the media, and this was especially prevalent in Britain in the 1970s. As film funding became scarcer, directors such as Stephen Frears and Ken Loach preferred to focus their attentions on television, leading to the popular expression 'British cinema is alive and well and living on television'.[19] But in the 1980s this evolved into a direct partnership, as Channel 4 began funding film productions, which in turn influenced ITV and the BBC to cultivate their own film financing activities. This opened up a debate about the implications of this new development for the film industry in Britain, and at the centre of this debate was the issue of whether these productions were films or simply 'jumped up single plays'. In 1984, Jeremy Isaacs summed up the problem: 'some people argue that films made on this scale are neither one thing nor the other; too slight for the cinema, too slack for television'.[20] While many critics saw the benefit of television funding to an ailing film industry, others questioned what this might mean for the types of production emerging from this partnership. They argued that making films with television money, for screening on television, might lead to a scaling down of the cinematic imagination (and further exacerbate the diversion of talent and resources from independent film production).

This culminated in arguments regarding the essential differences between cinema and television at the level of visual style. Television drama, linked to notions of Public Service Broadcasting (even for commercial broadcasters), has been influenced by theatrical and literary sensibilities, and, according to Martin McLoone, 'naturalism [has been] its defining aesthetic'. He argued that while many of the plays of the 1970s were shot on film, the artistic potential of these productions was never fully realised because of long-held values of British TV drama production which 'failed to see the celluloid through the script'.[21] Indeed, Martyn Auty argues that publicists, reviewers and filmmakers were shy of using the term 'TV movie' to describe Films on Four because of the negative connotations of this term. From the 1960s, the BBC had been producing 'plays' on film, while the Hollywood 'TV movie' was popularly seen as being 'formulaic' and suited only to the small screen.[22] Excessive 'literariness' was an accusation often levelled at British cinema generally, but particularly at Film on Four, which was seen as evolving out of the single-play tradition. Directors like Lindsay Anderson worried that the channel's involvement in British cinema might lead to distinctly 'uncinematic' filmmaking:

> I think the real difference is the kind of subject liable to be financed by Channel 4, which leads to some of the new British films being a bit lacking in the ambition one associated with a cinema film. There is a certain restriction of imagination or idea, rather than the feeling that if you make a film financed by television you have to restrict it in terms of technique or style.[23]

There was also the stigma of making a production with television funding, which could make it seem less attractive to distributors and cinemagoers. As a result, in the early days of Film on Four, producers and distributors tended to play down the television angle. Nicholas Mellersh of Rediffusion (which partly funded Mike Radford's 1983 film *Another Time, Another Place*) was of the opinion that there should be no mention of Channel 4 involvement when films were being distributed, stating that reviews which proclaimed 'another breakthrough hit for Channel 4' meant that it was 'not surprising that nobody goes to see the film'.[24]

Common arguments, in addition to ideas about aesthetic differences, also related to viewing space and the 'flow' of television. Ken Loach, who was to secure major commissions for the channel in the early 1990s, saw television as the enemy of film:

> It is not the technology of television that is at fault, rather the use that is made of it – it is visual wallpaper, a sort of McDonalds of the mind, which reduces a film enormously and to some extent is extremely destructive because of the fragmented way it is seen. Chased off the screen by a different set of images and then preceded by another set of images, the film becomes very much diminished as a coherent entity.[25]

Furthermore, a darkened auditorium filled with hundreds of people allowed undivided attention, whereas in a sitting room television had to compete with everyday life, with the remote control allowing the freedom to flick back and forth. This is of course a problem inherent with viewing any film on television, however, and most criticisms directed at Films on Four were less about the obvious differences between television and film and more about how television financing would affect the aesthetics of British film productions. What this essential difference actually *was* is difficult to pinpoint. What constitutes a television film and how does it differ from a 'cinema' film? This question generated vague arguments such as Mamoun Hassan's assertion that 'television is at its best explaining and describing'.[26] In 1984, Penelope Houston, editor of *Sight and Sound*, wrote:

> No one wants to look the Channel 4 gift-horse in the mouth … but … there remains a nagging feeling that what we've got … isn't quite enough: that the movie movie, as opposed to the TV movie, enjoys not only a wider vitality, but the power to probe more deeply.[27]

There have also been (and continue to be) debates surrounding the long-term effects of television funding on the industry. In 1995, David Elstein, Head of Programming for BSkyB, submitted evidence to the National Heritage Committee suggesting that television funding led producers and directors to make films which were less likely to appeal to cinema audiences, stating that

> there is no long term future in the £1–3m business. That is what has been the bane of the European film industry. It has been locked into the low-budget mode for decades while Hollywood has been sweeping up the pool by reinvesting in the film industry.[28]

Underlying the above criticisms was the desire for British producers to make films that could compete with the Hollywood studios in domestic and international markets, an idea which has long been suggested in government policy documents relating to the film industry. However, it has been the case that whenever British cinema has tried to make an impact in the US market, the industry has been unable to sustain costly failures because it does not have the infrastructure to engage in filmmaking on this scale.

David Rose tended not to distinguish between films for the cinema and films for television. Part of the reluctance to decide what might make a good cinema or television film stemmed from the fact that the channel so often got it wrong. For example, some films made with the cinema in mind could collapse, while films made purely for television might attract a theatrical release.[29] *My Beautiful Laundrette*, though 'strictly a film for television',[30] became one of the most successful productions financed by Channel 4 in the 1980s. The film gained a theatrical run in the UK following favourable reception at the Edinburgh Film and Television Festival, and also managed to secure North American distribution. However, in general, Films on Four were not expected to make any returns in the domestic market, and as a result sales to international markets became an increasingly crucial source of revenue.

As the channel began to develop strategies for launching films in the international art-house market, Head of Sales Larry Coyne urged filmmakers to 'consider adding those extra features – sound quality, widescreen and camera movement among them – that will help to make it attractive to the theatrical market'.[31] According to Coyne, it took filmmakers and the channel a few years to realise what might work in the cinema:

> we are now doing things that we didn't do three years ago; we shoot on 35mm in a widescreen ratio and we sometimes pay for stereo sound. These things are unimportant if you're producing a TV film but important if you're trying to impress a cinema audience.[32]

It is unsurprising that Coyne, who was responsible for selling Films on Four where the channel owned the rights to do so, would encourage filmmakers to make their productions more appealing to cinemagoers. However, this illustrates that even among Channel 4 personnel, views differed regarding those qualities which made a film 'cinematic'. This also shows that making films for cinema release (which necessitated being able to secure the interest of distributors) was a learning process for both the channel and filmmakers.

The aesthetic preoccupation with the difference between films made for television as well as cinema was a distinctively British concern, given the close association of Films on Four with the single play, and the strong theatrical and literary tradition evident in British television drama. Elsewhere in Europe, television had been a source of finance for film production for many years, but British cinema could draw upon no such precedent. This became increasingly apparent with the channel's involvement in international film festivals. At festivals like Cannes, for example, Films on Four tended not to be viewed as television films. In 1983, David Aukin stated that:

> This is a debate you would only have in the UK. In France, Germany, in the US, they don't know what they're talking about. Clearly if you don't have a huge budget you cannot make epic movies, but it's the grammar of *filmmaking* … In no sense is *Naked* a television film, it is a proper movie, for the big or small screen. Look at Peter Weir's *Green Card* … If you took away the stars … there is nothing left to say that it's a big film.[33]

Films on Four, then, initially had to contend with a significant amount of historical baggage, influenced by the long history and socially conscious traditions of Public Service Broadcasting. This is further evidenced when we consider the wide variety of films sponsored by the channel. While realist dramas dealing with contemporary issues like Karl Francis's *Giro City* (1982) and Joseph Despins' *The Disappearance of Harry* (1983) seemed to fit firmly into the single-play aesthetic, films like Wim Wenders' *Paris, Texas* (1984), Neil Jordan's *The Company of Wolves* (1984), Mike Newell's *Dance with a Stranger* (1985) and Peter Greenaway's *The Draughtsman's Contract* (1982) were associated with the 'cinematic'.

The debate around television funding drew out prejudices from all sides, and this prejudice arose partly from unrealistic expectations regarding the kinds of productions that the British film industry should be expected to make, and partly from preconceived associations between Films on Four and the television play. In reality, the canon of Films on Four in this era is too diverse and varied to attempt to apply a blanket 'cinema' or 'television' label.

Film on Four as a broadcast strand

Although in secondary literature (and throughout this book) the term 'Film on Four' is used to denote the channel's film commissioning activities, between 1982 and 1998 Film on Four was also a broadcast strand on which the films were screened, and the broadcast strand was not always synonymous with the channel's funding and co-production practices. Not all of the feature films funded by the channel were shown on the strand, and not all Films on Four were funded by the Drama Department. For example, the Multicultural Department funded Mira Nair's 1988 film *Salaam Bombay*, while the Education Department funded Derek Jarman's *Wittgenstein* (1993). Alan Fountain's Independent Film and Video Department could also fund a number of feature films each year, and the film buying department could also pre-buy the television rights to productions on occasion, as they did with Palace Pictures' *The Pope Must Die* (Peter Richardson, 1991) and with Working Title's *Map of the Human Heart* (Vincent Ward, 1993). The Film on Four strand could also be used to promote the channel's other filmmaking activities, as it did in Autumn 1989, Autumn 1990 and Summer 1992, when its usual slot was expressly given over to the Independent Film and Video Department in order to celebrate their considerable contribution to filmmaking. The popularity of the strand was here used as a beacon of prestige, in order to publicise the channel's wider efforts.

The core business of showcasing specially commissioned new feature films provides a valuable index of the changes over time in the channel's policy and identity as a film financier. For example, the first season of Film on Four shows the extent to which early Channel 4 films very much followed the style of the traditional single play for television. *Walter*, directed by Stephen Frears in 1982, was broadcast on the channel's first evening of transmission. It starred Ian McKellen as a disabled young man struggling to survive in an unsympathetic society, and in its subject matter and aesthetic, *Walter* followed very much in the tradition of the socially conscious single play. Walter is likened to a caged bird, something Frears emphasises with his use of extreme close-ups in small spaces, conjuring a sense of confinement that works well on the television screen but would not, one suspects, in the cinema. Michael Apted's *P'tang Yang Kipperbang* (1982), the second film screened in this first season of ten films, deals with a young boy coming to terms with his adolescence and was made as a small-scale film by Goldcrest specifically for television.

However, within a couple of years the channel had achieved considerable theatrical and critical successes with films like *My Beautiful Laundrette* and *Letter to Brezhnev*, and was also entering into high-profile international co-productions like *Paris Texas*. This was reflected in the channel's well-publicised 1987 Film on Four season. Promoted by the press as being Film on Four's 'most celebrated film season yet',[34] the films shown were very much representative of the different types of production that the channel had funded throughout the decade. Films like *Cal* (Pat O'Connor, 1984) and *No Surrender* (Peter Smith, 1985) dealt with the political situation in Ireland, while *Letter to Brezhnev* and *The Chain* (Jack Gold, 1984) engaged with social issues. *She'll Be Wearing Pink Pyjamas* and *The Assam Garden* (Mary McMurray, 1985) dealt with themes of acceptance and personal growth, while *Another Country* (Marek Kanievska, 1984) provided an example of the kinds of glossy costume drama reminiscent of films like Merchant Ivory's *A Room with a View* and Mike Newell's *Dance with a Stranger*. *My Beautiful Laundrette* was a politically conscious film originally made exclusively for television, but was recognised as offering impressive visual originality and a fresh approach to issues like race and homosexuality, while Derek Jarman's *Caravaggio* (1986) and Peter Greenaway's *A Zed and Two Noughts* (1986) represented the channel's consistent support for experimental directors. This season also included strange curios which did not seem to fit into any particular tradition. *The Company of Wolves*, a cult film based on a fairytale which drew stylistically upon the films of Michael Powell and Emeric Pressburger, seemed startlingly out of place in the British cinema of the early 1980s. *Billy the Kid and the Green Baize Vampire* (Alan Clarke, 1987), a musical about a young boy who takes on the world snooker champion, was not successful, although the fact that this unconventional film was commissioned in the first place is notable. The season was well publicised in Channel 4's weekly Press Information Packs, and gained the channel its highest ever viewing figures in Film on Four's history. And as the channel's 1988 Annual Report was keen to point out, this was 'mostly for films in which the style or content was more controversial, like *Letter to Brezhnev*'.[35]

The publicity surrounding this season reflects the significance of Film on Four within the channel's wider cultural remit. In 1985, Justin Dukes stated in an internal policy document that Film on Four was important to the channel because it achieved good audience figures, represented the support of a broadcaster for British film, and also represented a revitalisation of the low-budget scale of British filmmaking.[36] The profitability of Film on Four was apparently not a pressing problem. Around 7% of the channel's annual budget went towards Film on Four, which meant that the channel was spending approximately one-twelfth of its budget making just twenty programmes out of a total of 3,000 hours of programming.[37] In 1983 Jeremy Isaacs admitted that this was problematic, but stated that, 'on the other hand, these things have a socio-cultural provenance and purpose, as well as being simply a contribution to the ratings'.[38] Film on Four was also seen as important in garnering awards and critical acclaim for the channel, through theatrical release and participation in festivals. Between 1982 and 1985, thirty-four of the sixty films funded through Film on Four had cinema screenings, and twenty-five of those films had received awards and been selected for film festivals. According to Dukes, 'all of this has greatly enhanced the channel's public image as a responsible and creative ingredient in British broadcasting'.[39]

The end of Film on Four?

Channel 4 effectively created the identity of the Film on Four strand through the structuring of its seasons and through the publicity surrounding those seasons, and this was influenced by the critical reception and box-office success garnered by each production. In the mid-to-late 1980s the channel also began screening repeat seasons of Film on Four under the titles of Take Two and Film on Four Extra, and an analysis of these seasons provides insight into what the channel considered to be its most successful and culturally influential films. In January 1993, the channel screened a repeat season entitled 'Film on Four's Greatest Hits' to mark the tenth anniversary of the strand. The Channel 4 Season Information Packs stated: 'This season features 13 of the most popular and successful Film on Four's to have emerged over the past decade which proves how closely Channel 4 has been associated with the biggest recent successes of the British film industry.'[40] The season was indeed representative of the diversity of successful films funded by the Drama Department, ranging from the obvious choices to more obscure vehicles. Also included were John Boorman's *Hope and Glory* (1987), Stephen Frears's *Prick Up Your Ears* (1987), Mike Newell's *Dance with a Stranger* and Terence Davies' more experimental *Distant Voices, Still Lives* (1988).[41]

However, David Aukin argues that there was perhaps a hint of desperation behind this celebration of Film on Four's achievements. The strand went through an 18-month hiatus between 1990 and 1991, as David Rose departed and David Aukin took over as Head of Drama. This meant that the channel did not have much to show, and few of the films being released were having much of an impact.[42] Between 1990 and 1993, the Film on Four budget was also cut by 10%, remaining steady at £11 million for three years.[43] More generally, the country and by extension the film industry was suffering through a worldwide economic recession. Added to this malaise, Aukin stated that there were very few fresh and innovative projects to match even Film on Four's relatively small budget: 'Do I have enough good projects in hand to justify making films? Although I have some, I don't have enough. I'm not just going to fill quotas.'[44] The viability of theatrical release was also an issue, and following a disappointing experience with Ken Loach's *Riff-Raff* (1991), which failed to secure decent exhibition in the UK, Aukin was reconsidering releasing Film on Four films in cinemas.[45]

For these reasons, Aukin considered diverting money from Film on Four to other areas such as video plays, drama series and single drama.[46] Maggie Brown argues that it was Chief Executive Michael Grade's deep personal dislike of the strand that led to consideration of it being axed. She writes: 'he saw it as vanity publishing, there to make the channel look good rather than to garner ratings', and argues that he was eventually won round by the considerable success of *Shallow Grave*, thereafter adopting something of a 'movie mogul' persona.[47] However, the situation was not clear-cut, although the channel had to some extent lost confidence in Film on Four. Aukin states:

> When I started it was made clear to me that Film [on] Four was not sacrosanct, and that if I thought it should be abandoned … the channel would have been very happy. So I said 'well let me assess it'. And I did and after 6 or 7 months I came back and said 'No I think there's nothing wrong with the vase, it's just the flowers need to be differently arranged. The talent is there, and we've got the right vehicle to engage that talent'. I don't think that went down well with the channel [laughs].[48]

For the first two or three years of Aukin's tenure, Film on Four was effectively on trial.[49] However, this was less to do with Michael Grade's own dislike of the strand than with extenuating circumstances. After 1993, the channel found itself under pressure in an era that saw the expansion of satellite channels and the new fifth channel, meaning that it had to adhere to its remit to be innovative and original yet still be able to attract advertisers. As Ellis Cashmore argues:

> Market forces traditionally lead to imitation, not originality. Channel 4's dilemma was compounded by the fact that it was and still is

> ostensibly non-profit making. Yet it has to swim in the same waters
> as overtly commercial stations when it bids for advertisers' money.[50]

The channel faced the unusual position of being a commercial broadcaster that had to react to the pressures of the market while adhering to the public service requirements set out in the 1980 and 1990 Broadcasting Acts.[51] In this new commercial environment, Channel 4 television executives had an uneasy relationship with film. They had little interest in it, according to Aukin, because of the three-year holdback between theatrical release and television broadcast for larger-budget films. They also naturally had more interest in television, and because Film on Four had not achieved any great successes during this hiatus period, there was a feeling that its greatest days were over.[52] There was also a feeling of uncertainty as to whether the channel could survive through selling its own advertising, and Film on Four had to prove itself in this new commercial market.

Theatrical success in a competitive broadcasting era

Aukin cites *Shallow Grave* as being 'the film that turned the tide'[53] as the first Film on Four in years to recoup its costs at the domestic box office. Catherine Johnson argues that in the 1990s broadcasters like the BBC and Channel 4 began to utilise branding strategies as a means of survival in the new commercial market.[54] From 1997 to 2001, Chief Executive Michael Jackson consciously conceived of the broadcaster as a brand to be exploited in the rapidly changing media market, launching a number of digital subscription channels such as FilmFour and E4.[55] During Michael Grade's tenure, the channel's brand identity was not as consciously exploited in the same way, but there had always been elements of Channel 4's programming which it endeavoured to promote as being a distinctive part of its identity. According to Aukin, following the huge commercial successes of films like *Shallow Grave, Four Weddings and a Funeral* and *Trainspotting*:

> [Film on Four] became part of the branding of Channel 4, in the
> same way as Channel 4 News, they didn't have *Big Brother* then,
> but there are certain things that branded Channel 4, and Film Four
> became one of those.[56]

Film on Four had already developed a distinctive identity over the years, which allowed the channel to exploit the cultural prestige of the strand as part of its overall remit to provide distinctive and innovative programming. However, this suggests that after the commercial successes of the mid-1990s Film on Four became part of the channel's 'brand' identity more than ever before.

It was perhaps because of this success that the mid-1990s saw an increased commitment to British cinema on the part of the channel. Michael Grade was especially keen to emphasise the value of Film on Four to the channel, helping the latter fulfil its PSB requirements. In 1996, Grade wrote:

> The main purpose of Film on Four remains to help fulfil the basic remit with which the channel was charged in the 1981 Broadcasting Act, and which was maintained verbatim in the 1990 Act: to provide the most distinctive and innovative dramatic work that we can for our viewers at home.[57]

He also stressed that profit was not the motivation for funding films, because even a film as commercially successful as *Four Weddings and a Funeral* would only contribute £3–4 million to a broadcaster with a turnover of over £300 million per year.[58] The worldwide success of *Four Weddings* brought the channel something much greater than profit: prestige, and a widespread recognition of Channel 4's commitment to British cinema.

This commitment was partly symptomatic of greater competition and the increasing need to retain the channel's considerable yearly turnover. When the channel began selling its own advertising, safety measures were put in place in the event that it failed to support itself. If the channel dipped below 14% of the total advertising revenue, ITV would step in and provide 2%. If the channel went above 14%, this would be divided equally between Channel 4 and the ITV companies.[59] However, after the transition the channel performed extremely well, which meant that in 1993 it was required to hand over £38 million to ITV, and in 1994 £55 million.[60] Grade lobbied the Department of National Heritage (DNH), arguing that the current system was unnecessary and that it should be dropped to allow the channel to divert more money into programming – specifically, to Film on Four. As an incentive to the DNH Grade pledged to double the budget of Film on Four if the system was dropped, a measure which he stated could boost the film industry and create 1,000 jobs. He argued that:

> Channel 4 is committed to film in a way that no-one else has been and we would dearly love to continue that support. Film lies at the

> core of our remit and was the only area of programming on which
> we made the case for changing the funding formula.[61]

In 1996 the government reduced the amount of revenue that the channel was obliged to pay to ITV and set a cap on the reserve fund which acted as a safety net, allowing the channel to keep an extra £35 million per year and allowing Grade to increase the budget of Film on Four to £22 million in 1997.[62]

The channel was also facing competition over pay-tv rights. In 1995, it became embroiled in a bitter battle with BSkyB following a deal with British Screen which stated that BSkyB could invest in a certain number of British Screen films in return for the rights to broadcast these productions on the Sky movie channels. Channel 4 was furious and ended its deal with British Screen as a result. Grade argued that if the channel had invested a considerable sum of money in a film, it should have the sole UK right to transmission:

> Holding back for a cinema release is one thing; waiting for a satellite competitor is another. If we're buying completed feature films, as broadcasters have long done, we'll wait our turn – behind cinema, video, satellite and cable. But not if we're investing in a major commissioned strand like Film on Four.[63]

It was for this reason that in its press publications the channel began to consistently and repeatedly emphasise the 'premiere' season between 1995 and 1998. The Autumn 1995 season packs announced 'the strongest Film on Four premiere season in the history of the channel',[64] while the 1997 packs introduced viewers to 'an exceptionally strong premiere season'.[65] In doing so, the channel sought to highlight the exclusivity of these films at a time of competing movie platforms.

Conclusion

Changes in Channel 4's film policy have been subject to a number of complex external factors, and the channel's relationship with the film industry has also evolved over time as a consequence. Film on Four had always served as a beacon of cultural prestige for the channel, although this was perhaps more prominent in the 1980s when the channel embodied a firm cultural remit and was not quite as concerned with the need to be financially self-sufficient. Between 1990 and 1993 we can identify a considerable amount of uncertainty on the part of the channel regarding its film policy, an uncertainty which was reflective of wider issues at that time – a worldwide recession, the deregulation of broadcasting, increased commercialism and the move towards selling its own advertising. However, the channel quickly became commercially self-sufficient, and sought to embrace the success of Film on Four following hits such as *Shallow Grave* and *Four Weddings and a Funeral*. The channel began to promote Film on Four as a prominent part of its identity, but also as an example of how it was continuing to fulfil its public service remit despite accusations of commercialism. At a time when there was significant doubt as to whether the channel could operate commercially and continue to retain its public service ideals, Film on Four was proof of the channel's ongoing commitment to British cinema, and the diversity of its film output also meant that it was catering to different tastes and audiences.

Film on Four has led a strange existence, being essentially a funder/producer of film while operating within a broadcasting environment. Like the BBC, which shortly followed in its wake, Channel 4 was a broadcaster dedicated to funding feature films. However, unlike the BBC, the channel's film arm operated with relative autonomy, and worked similarly to a film studio as well as being part of a larger organisation with a strong cultural remit. As a result, Channel 4's policy towards film was flexible, with Commissioning Editors David Rose and David Aukin afforded a significant amount of freedom to make the kinds of personal and instinctive judgements necessary in film production.

Notes

1. Stephen Woolley, interviewed by Laura Mayne and Justin Smith, 22 March 2012.
2. John Hill, *British Cinema in the 1980s: Issues and Themes* (Oxford: Clarendon Press, 1999), 54.
3. John Hill, 'British Television and Film: The Making of a Relationship?', in *Big Picture, Small Screen: The Relations Between Film and Television*, ed. by John Hill and Martin McLoone (Luton: University of Luton Press, 1996), 151–76, 153.
4. Hill, *British Cinema in the 1980s*, 31.
5. Hill, 'British Television and Film', in *Big Picture, Small Screen*, 157.
6. Hill, *British Cinema in the 1980s*, 61.
7. John Pym, 'Showman Grade Boosts Ratings, Riles Critics', *Screen International*, 11 November 1992.
8. Bryan Appleyard, 'Children of Channel 4', *Sunday Times Magazine*, 21 February 1988.
9. Anon., 'Another Time, Another Place', *Stills* (July 1983).

10.   KM, 'C4 Film Wait', *Broadcast*, 4 October 1982.

11.   BFI Special Collections, Papers of Roger Graef, CF Paper 215 (February 1984).

12.   KM, 'C4 Film Wait'.

13.   Anon., 'Channel 4 Face Dilemma', *Broadcast*, 1 February 1985.

14.   *Ibid.*

15.   British Screen Advisory Council, *Report on Activities 1 January 1986 to 31 May 1987* (London: BSAC, 1987).

16.   *Ibid.*

17.   Paul Webster, personal communication.

18.   Charles Barr, 'They Think it's all Over: The Dramatic Legacy of Live Television', in *Big Picture, Small Screen*, 50.

19.   Charlotte Brunsdon, '"It's a Film": Medium Specificity as Textual Gesture in Red Road and The Unloved', *Journal of British Cinema and Television*, 9:3 (2012), 457.

20.   Jeremy Isaacs, 'Life Before Death on Television', *Sight and Sound* (Spring 1984), 116.

21.   Martin McLoone, 'Boxed in? The Aesthetics of Film and Television', in *Big Picture, Small Screen*, 97.

22.   Martyn Auty, 'But Is It Cinema?', in *British Cinema Now*, ed. by Martyn Auty and Nick Roddick (London: BFI, 1985), 59.

23.   Paul Giles, 'History with Holes: Channel 4 Television Films of the 1980s', in *Fires Were Started: British Cinema and Thatcherism*, ed. by Lester Friedman, 2nd edn (Minneapolis: Minnesota University Press, 1993), 64.

24.   Anthony Hayward, 'Producers at Loggerheads over Films on Four', *Screen International*, 25 June 1983.

25.   Larry Coyne, 'TV used to feed off the cinema, now the reverse is true', *Broadcast*, 9 May 1986.

26.   Mamoun Hassan, 'Life before death on television', *Sight and Sound* (Spring 1984), 116.

27.   Hill, *British Cinema in the 1980s*, 63.

28.   House of Commons, National Heritage Committee, 'The British Film Industry: Second Report', Vol. 1 (1995).

29.   Hilary Brown, 'The Film Man', *Airwaves*, 13 (1987), 23–5.

30.   Philip Reevel, 'Films, Four, and Funding', *Televisual* (February 1985).

31.   Sebastian Taylor, 'C4 sales on target to reach 4m', *Broadcast*, 28 November 1986.

32.   Coyne, 'TV used to feed off the cinema'.

33.   Joanna Coles, 'Life in the Small Frame', *The Guardian*, 18 May 1993.

34.   *Daily Express*, 11 February 1987.

35.   Channel 4, *Annual Report and Accounts* (London: Channel 4 Television Corporation, 1987), 17.

36.   BFI Special Collections, Papers of Roger Graef, CF Paper 312, 'Film on Four' (1985).

37.   Stephen Lambert, 'Still Smiling: An Interview with Jeremy Isaacs', *Stills*, 6 (May–June 1983), 26.

38.   *Ibid.*, 26.

39.   Graef, 'Film on Four'.

40.   Channel 4 Press Packs, Season Information Pack (Winter 1993).

41. Channel 4 Press Packs, Season Information Pack (Spring 1987).

42. David Aukin, personal communication, 23 February 2012.

43. *Screen Finance*, 12 August 1992.

44. *Screen International*, 1 March 1991.

45. *Screen International*, 5 May 1995.

46. *Ibid.*

47. Maggie Brown, *A Licence to Be Different: The Story of Channel 4* (London: BFI Publishing, 2007), 188.

48. David Aukin, personal communication, 23 February 2012.

49. *Screen International*, 26 September 1997.

50. Ellis Cashmore, *... and Then There Was Television* (London: Routledge, 1994), 197.

51. John Ellis, 'Innovation in Form and Content?', in *The Television History Book*, ed. by Michele Hilmes (London: BFI Publishing, 2003), 98.

52. David Aukin, personal communication, 23 February 2012.

53. *Ibid.*

54. Catherine Johnson, *Branding Television* (London: Routledge, 2012).

55. Ellis, 'Innovation in Form and Content?', 97.

56. Aukin, 23 February 2012.

57. Michael Grade, 'Getting the Right Approach', in *Big Picture, Small Screen*, 179.

58. *Ibid.*, 179.

59. Sylvia Harvey, 'Channel 4 Television: From Annan to Grade', in *Behind the Screens: The Structure of British Television in the Nineties*, ed. by Stuart Hood (London: Lawrence and Wishart, 1994), 102–32, 127.

60. Anon., 'Grade vows to fight on over C4 funding formula', *Screen Finance*, 25 January 1995, 5.

61. *Ibid.*

62. *Screen Finance*, 21 February 1996, 7.

63. Grade, 'Getting the Right Approach', 179.

64. Channel 4 Press Packs, Season Information Pack (Autumn 1995).

65. Channel 4 Press Packs, Season Information Pack (Autumn 1997).

Chapter 4

The aesthetics of early Film on Four

Films on Four cannot easily be grouped in terms of style or genre, and many of the early titles were criticised for being a strange breed, with little consistency between them. The filmmaker James Scott commented that 'they could have come from anywhere, even dropped from the moon', adding that 'they don't relate to very much, and show no awareness of cinema tradition'.[1] Early Films on Four can be seen as having close links to the television play, but in fact they also draw influences from a variety of sources. Perhaps they 'showed no awareness of cinema tradition' because they were something new: films which employed hybridised forms and borrowed aesthetics drawn from a broad range of filmmaking styles and genres. Derek Malcolm, writing for *The Guardian* in 1983, points to how British film critics were attempting to quantify the ways in which British film culture was rapidly changing due to the arrival of Channel 4:

> 'What are the emerging themes and styles of the new British cinema?' asked an Italian critic at the Taormina Festival the other week after Mike Radford's *Another Time, Another Place* had become the second British film in successive years to win the festival's top prize. No one knew quite how to answer the question since there seems very little contact between *The Draughtsman's Contract* and *Ascendancy*, or *Angel* and *Local Hero*. Even *Another Time, Another Place* and *Remembrance*, the two Taormina winners, could scarcely be further apart.[2]

The evolution of Film on Four in the 1980s coincided with the emergence of new aesthetic trends in British cinema, trends which have been identified elsewhere by Christopher Williams, John Hill and Paul Giles.[3] For example, Williams argues that many Films on Four seemed to merge the 'traditional' social-realist aspects of British cinema with the more personal and 'subjective' concerns of European art cinema, spawning a number of productions which fall into the category of what he terms 'Social Art Cinema', an idea which was later expanded upon by

Samantha Lay.[4] This idea of European styles merging with British had its industrial determinants in a need for more specialised and international exhibition, as well as Channel 4's increasing involvement in European co-productions throughout the decade. Paul Giles argues that the Channel 4 films of the 1980s 'deal more convincingly with confinement than escape'. However, Giles also noted the ways in which Films on Four such as *Wish You Were Here* and *The Ploughman's Lunch* (Richard Eyre, 1983) offered intelligent, self-conscious critiques of the past. This can be seen as part of a wider trend in the 1980s towards self-reflexive, personal histories, a feature noted by Amy Sargeant.[5] This chapter will deal with some of these ideas, questioning how far these emerging styles can be seen as being, in some ways, a result of the involvement of Channel 4 in the film culture of this period.

Space, place and the regional

What is notable about many early Channel 4 films of the 1980s is their strong preoccupation with regional areas of the UK. Twenty-one of the sixty-six Films on Four transmitted between 1982 and 1987 were filmed in regions outside London and the South East, including the North of England, Scotland, Wales and Ireland. Among the most identifiable aspects of the first commissioned Films on Four were rural settings, and these account for ten of these twenty-one films. In many of these productions, the central characters seem firmly bonded to the landscape and indeed the landscape almost seems to play a major character. Michael Radford's *Another Time, Another Place* and Bill Bryden's *Ill Fares the Land* (1983) are typical of this category. Six of these films are set in regional urban centres and deal with themes such as poverty, confinement and urban depression, and tend to foreground plucky characters set against a grey and miserable working-class England. These films have been seen to draw their influences directly from the British New Wave films of the 1959–1963 period: films such as Chris Bernard's *Letter to Brezhnev* and Alan Clarke's *Rita, Sue and Bob Too* seem strongly connected to this era of British cinema.

Despite Rose's professed dislike of adaptations and of Second World War films, there were no hard and fast rules at Film on Four.[6] Indeed Michael Radford's *Another Time, Another Place* became a personal favourite of Rose's because 'it did what we were trying to do in Birmingham' in creating an authentic view of a particular community.[7] Based on a semi-autobiographical novel by Jessie Kesson, *Another Time* is set on the Black

Isle, just north of Inverness, and tells the story of Janey (Phyllis Logan), who falls in love with one of the Italian prisoners of war stationed in her village during World War Two. The film was critically acclaimed for its poetic realism and its use of landscape, which seemed to draw upon European rather than British cinematic traditions. In this film, the Isle is all-encompassing and oppressive: the setting is used to emphasise a stifling claustrophobia which is almost expressionist, reflecting Janey's entrapment in her marriage and her homeland. Numerous landscape shots make the ground and sky seem far too close together. In the words of one reviewer, 'glowering lurid skies [are] hung so low one feels the characters will have to crawl beneath them', which leads to feelings of oppression rather than the sense of freedom associated with wide open spaces.[8] The poignant melancholy of the film lies in the fact that, in spite of her desire to escape, Janey is firmly bonded to the island just as much as her lover is bonded to Naples. Janey's Italian has shown her that there are other times and other places but that she will probably never see them.

Andrew Higson argues that cinematic space 'is always at some level invested with value, meaning, and significance, whether that meaning is generated internally by the interplay of characters, events, and filmic presentation, or extratextually by the connotations those spaces have for audiences'.[9] In many early commissioned Films on Four, rural landscapes often seem to interact with the narrative at some level,

Figure 4.1 *Another Time, Another Place*

sometimes almost functioning as characters in their own right. In Bill Bryden's *Ill Fares the Land*, the landscape acts as both a nourishing and a constraining force. Filmed in Applecross in Wester-Ross, *Ill Fares the Land* tells the story of the residents of the island of St Kilda in the Outer Hebrides and their tough decision to leave their remote home for the Scottish mainland. The film portrays a beautiful but untameable landscape of oppositions. Shots of the landscape, of the cliffs of the island jutting into the sky and of waves crashing onto the shore, emphasise its rugged beauty, but this is as much harsh and fickle as aesthetically pleasing. In its depiction of the island the film recalls Michael Powell's god-like representation of St Kilda in his 1937 film *The Edge of the World*; in *Ill Fares the Land*, the island gives life but it also takes life away, and this is ultimately why the villagers must leave their perfect society for life on the mainland. Throughout the film, the camera moves with painstaking slowness, drawing the viewer in to the pace of village life and contrasting with the fast-moving lives of those who leave for the mainland to find work. The stark dichotomy between modern culture and the islanders' way of life is shown in detail when tourists visit the island for a taste of genuine rural Scottish culture and end up ransacking it in their enthusiasm, leaving the villagers with a flu virus which their immune systems are ill-equipped to deal with. As the forces of modernity unwittingly obliterate the natural equilibrium of the community, the islanders are unceremoniously ripped out of time and place and led confused and bewildered into a new life to which they cannot adapt.

As Annie Morgan James argues, images of Scotland on film are often associated with rural landscapes and the myths connected to those landscapes,[10] while Ireland is also often portrayed on film as a rural utopia removed from the modern world.[11] Such depictions predominate in early Films on Four. In 1983 Steve McIntyre criticised such representations, arguing that by romanticising an 'apolitical' national identity they served the ideological function of displacing and preventing other representations that might have had some actual political significance.[12] These films may indeed represent a form of escapism from modern life by hankering after a nostalgic past, but one can also identify in these productions a sort of re-assertion of cultural identity and a reifying of regional 'place' in national cinema. This preoccupation with place even caught the attention of American critics. In 1986, a season of early Films on Four was shown on PBS, which included Michael Darlow's

Accounts and Colin Gregg's *Remembrance*. The *New York Times* critic John O'Connor noted that

> unlike most American made-for-television movies, which could be taking place in just about any suburban setting across the United States ... their British counterparts are rooted in unmistakably specific locations. From the opening scene, there can be no doubt that *Accounts* is taking place in Scotland.[13]

This suggests that early Film on Four productions held an appeal which was very much rooted in cultural specificity.

History from below?

Films on Four set in rural Ireland tend to focus predominantly on agrarian and sometimes mythical pasts. Shot on location in one of the Irish 'ghost famine' villages, *The Outcasts* (1984), directed by Robert Wynne-Simmons, tells the story of Maura, a painfully awkward girl who becomes involved with a strange fiddler whose music causes fear and hallucinations wherever it is heard. Other rural Irish films deal specifically with relationships and personal memory, such as Paul Joyce's *Summer Lightning* (1984), which is set in County Wicklow just before the potato famine of 1845–52 and based around the reflections of an old man remembering his childhood. Rather than focusing on larger national histories, many of the rural films commissioned in the early years of Film on Four tend to favour looking to the past in order to explore personal relationships and the ways in which characters interact with 'place' and with landscapes of home. Amy Sargeant argues that the engagement with the past in the cinema of the 1980s was more about 'history from underneath', and that rather than focusing on national leaders and events, these portrayals of history tend to rely on personal memory and how such memories relate to the present day.[14]

In 1986, Paul Kerr noticed an emerging trend in British cinema in the form of increasing numbers of films dealing not just with personal histories, but histories which tended to focus on 'anti-heroes'. These were not biopics or national histories, but rather histories from the fringes which depicted the upper classes in unflattering terms. Examples include films like *Prick Up Your Ears* (1987), *Wish You Were Here*, *Comrades* (Bill Douglas, 1986), and *Dance with a Stranger* (1985).[15] The success of *Chariots of Fire* (Hugh Hudson, 1981) may have encouraged this trend towards more personal 'forgotten histories', but Kerr also cites institutional grounds:

> One [reason] is the increasing interdependence of film and television, an interdependence which inevitably results in a mixture between the two media's most familiar narrative forms: TV naturalism and current affairs formats fusing with cinema's larger than life fictions.[16]

Here it might appear that the convergence of cinema and television led to new cinematic trends, with British cinema engaging with forgotten histories which were intimate and dealt with personal memory in a critical way. With the exception of lavish costume dramas like *A Room with a View* which fetishise a particular view of British history, there is a definite immediacy to many of these Films on Four which encourages the viewer to relate to characters on a personal level but also to engage with the nature of memory and the ways in which the past is constructed. These are films which, while visually interesting, also seem especially suited to the direct and more intimate nature of television viewing. For example, *Prick Up Your Ears*, about the relationship between playwright Joe Orton and his lover Kenneth Halliwell, explores the emotional tensions between the

Figure 4.2   *Prick Up Your Ears*

couple and at times borders on melodrama. However, critical distance is encouraged through flashback sequences, alternating between the present (the film is framed by sequences of John Lahr researching the book on which it is based) and the past, exploring the ways in which the past can be constructed through interviews and eyewitness testimony. The viewer is invited into the action through direct speeches to camera on the part of Halliwell, who complains about his lover and attempts to explain his actions.

Richard Eyre's *The Ploughman's Lunch* is perhaps the best example of this type of production. The title comes from the popular dish, which, the film suggests, was invented by pub landlords to evoke nostalgic ideas of a national past in order to increase sales of cheese. The entire film is a commentary on the ways in which the past can be fictionalised to serve the agenda of those presently in power. One of the earliest Films on Four, Mike Hodges' *Squaring the Circle* (1983) even begins with the title card: 'everything you are about to see is true, except for the words and the pictures'.[17] As Paul Giles argues, *Wish You Were Here* also represents the past from the vantage point of the 1980s, with references to fish-and-chip stands and photographs of Gracie Fields evoking shared communal memories, but in a way that encourages analysis.[18] These films are almost hybrids, intimate but dealing with larger themes, evoking nostalgia but encouraging critical viewer engagement, commenting on national issues but (in many cases) remaining apathetic or apolitical. Yet these films were not produced in a vacuum, and one can note aesthetic influences on them beyond the televisual.

New Wave influences

Despite James Scott's claim that Films on Four showed 'no awareness of cinema tradition', early productions contained similarities with the location-shot tradition that started with the British New Wave, with its roots within the documentary movement of the 1930s and 1940s and Free Cinema in the 1950s. 'New Wave' was the name given to a series of films produced between 1959 and 1963 which were often shot on location in industrial towns in the Midlands or the North of England. Predominantly middle class and hailing from the south, New Wave directors were interested in including representations of the working class beyond London and utilised particular visual styles to portray the regions authentically, styles which became unfairly labelled as 'drab', 'gritty' and 'kitchen sink realism'. The idea of bringing a genuine sense of place to national cinema was therefore not a new one. However, whereas many New Wave directors sought to 'explore the exotic within the national'[19] by focusing on a working-class regional life as a way of elucidating that culture to an educated southern middle class, the productions Rose commissioned eschewed the framework of British national identity in favour of regional ones. Although the social context and production processes were vastly different, New Wave influences can be seen both in the location-shot dramas and series of Pebble Mill and in the regional films Rose commissioned at Channel 4.

This can particularly be seen in the category of urban, regional Films on Four identified earlier in this chapter, and of these productions Chris Bernard's *Letter to Brezhnev* in particular would seem to be closest to this tradition. In *Brezhnev* two working-class Liverpudlian girls seek a brief escape from boredom and a lack of opportunity by spending a night on the town with two visiting Russian sailors. The establishing shot marks out the cityscape and gradually zooms in until we find ourselves on a boat with Piotr and Sergei as they stare at the city in anticipation. Shots like these seem to hark back to the so-called 'Long Shot of Our Town from That Hill' convention of the New Wave films, which Higson notes often served as a romanticised 'spectacle', creating a 'pleasurable lure' for the viewer.[20]

Figure 4.3   *Letter to Brezhnev*

However, in *Brezhnev* this is shown to be self-consciously ironic, as the cultural references that Sergei associates with the Liverpool landscape ('Look! Liverpool! Beatles!') are at odds with the modern culture of Liverpudlian life. This is not the glamorous world of British pop, but the drab, unglamorous world of the chicken factory and the dole queue. And whereas in the location-shot, urban films of the New Wave community was often conveyed based on shared employment and location, Hill notes that in *Brezhnev* the decline of the working class is instead associated with unemployment and the collapse of heavy industry.[21] *Letter to Brezhnev* thus harks back to the stylistic tendencies of the New Wave, but also seems to be consciously at odds with that tradition.

The film was criticised for its lack of focus on the rich texture of Liverpool street life and the superfluity of its many establishing shots. One reviewer argues that 'the camera could have given us a more penetrating look. There are just too many establishing shots of the city's Victorian skyline, and the one montage of its prime tourist sites feels like a throwaway'.[22] But if the establishing shots do seem throwaway, of real interest here are shots of bleak, run-down council houses, peeling brown wallpaper and the stifling atmosphere of family arguments in tiny flats. Alan Clarke's *Rita, Sue and Bob Too* deals with similar themes, with two young Yorkshire girls seeking pleasure and thrills against a depressing urban backdrop. As in *Brezhnev*, familiarity is repressive and is perhaps best represented when Sue and her boyfriend Aslam endure an uncomfortable family visit in Sue's cramped, grimy flat. In both films we can identify a strong fatalism in relation to regional identity.

Samantha Lay observed of many New Wave films that 'character and place were often linked to explore some aspect of contemporary life'.[23] Trapped in a depressing community, Rita and Sue embark on an affair with a married man in order to keep the boredom and squalor of daily life at bay, but leaving that community is never even considered. In *Letter to Brezhnev*, Elaine escapes to Russia while Theresa is left at the airport gazing longingly after her. Elaine can leave because she is 'not like other Kirkby girls' with her exotic aspirations, but Theresa is 'a Kirkby girl through and through', and her sense of belonging to that community is so strong that she can never break away. The key difference between these films and those of the New Wave is that although character and place are strongly linked, in *Brezhnev* and *Rita* this link deals more with exploring the ways in which place relates to personal identity than any rallying cry for political change. As Lay observes of *Letter to Brezhnev*, the film is 'about never giving up, but this message is addressed to the individual and therefore not an appeal to the embattled working-class people of Liverpool or Britain. *Letter to Brezhnev* is a political film, but on a personal level.'[24] This foregrounding of the personal against a background of wider societal themes is a thread that runs throughout the Films on Four of the 1980s, and particularly in the films discussed in the following section.

The new 'Social Art Cinema'

Channel 4 funded a large percentage of the British films produced in the 1980s, and the convergence of cinema and television undoubtedly had an effect on the narratives and aesthetic style of British cinema in this era. Channel 4 was responsible for a renaissance in British filmmaking predominantly at the low-budget end of the market, funding films which tended to appeal to the independent circuit in Britain, and, as has been noted, to European art-house markets. In Britain, Channel 4 films existed in the market between large-budget studio productions and European art films. Indeed, Larry Coyne believed that, after the first few years of Film on Four, the channel had begun to produce a certain kind of film, the 'gritty low budget film', which appealed to a gap between the Hollywood and European markets.[25] Historically, this has been symptomatic of low-budget British filmmaking more generally. For example, Christopher Williams has argued that

> British cinema is caught between Hollywood and Europe, unconfident of its own identity, unable to commit or develop strongly in either direction. On one side an economically and artistically powerful industry … on the other a number of national cinemas which no longer have strong industrial bases but do in some cases represent perceptible senses of national identity.[26]

Throughout the 1980s Channel 4 was forced to negotiate this space for industrial reasons. A lack of UK government subsidy and a scarcity of American finance made European co-productions increasingly common, while the US dominance of major distribution circuits in Britain and Europe meant that most Films on Four could hope to achieve releases only on independent circuits. This section will argue that a struggle to achieve US funding and distribution and a growing relationship with Europe led, in many Films on Four, to a fusing of the traditional concerns of British low-budget filmmaking with the stylistic forms prevalent in European art cinema.

Christopher Williams attempts to categorise the Channel 4 films of the 1980s in terms of theme and visual style. For example, he states that of 138 Films on Four shown in the first ten years of the channel's operation, seventeen were concerned with political issues (for example, *The Ploughman's Lunch* and Pat O'Connor's *Cal* [1984]), sixteen seemed to take over from the serious, socially conscious concerns of the single play (e.g. Mike Newell's *The Good Father* [1985] and Jack Gold's *Good and Bad at Games* [1983]), nine were concerned with 'observational realism' (e.g. Mike Leigh's *Meantime* [1984]), nine addressed historical topics, and so on. However, Films on Four can be categorised endlessly. To illustrate, many of the regional films concerned with place discussed at the beginning of this chapter are also historical, political and socially conscious, and many also draw upon realist aesthetics. But Williams does note an interesting trend among the Films on Four of the 1980s, namely, the prevalence of the 'art' film, which constituted thirty-three (or 24%) of the 138 titles.[27] Examples include *Angel* (1982), *Caravaggio* (1986), *Distant Voices, Still Lives* (1988), *Moonlighting* (1982), *Letter to Brezhnev* and *My Beautiful Laundrette* (1985). All of these films address concerns evident in the European art film, characterised by Steve Neale as constituting a suppression of action, stress on character and 'a fore-grounding of style and authorial enunciation'.[28] The art film deals with issues of identity, foregrounding the personal over the social (and the social world is invariably alienating); it is ambiguous, more interested in character than plot, and often contains a distinctive visual style which may be associated with the authorship of the director.[29]

Williams goes on to argue that these films do not just align themselves stylistically with European art cinema; they also draw upon traditional elements of British cinema in their narratives. The result is a blend of realism and social concerns with a foregrounding of character and themes of social alienation. This can be seen in *Letter to Brezhnev*, which combines reflections on working-class life in Britain with personal narratives of love and feelings of isolation from family, friends and social institutions. *Angel* deals with a musician's desire to avenge the death of a young girl. His journey across the Irish countryside reveals his descent into madness and invites questions about the nature of violence and the human condition, but is also placed against the background of the Irish Troubles. But perhaps *My Beautiful Laundrette* provides the best example

Figure 4.4   *Angel*

of this blend of British social realism with art cinema. As Williams argues, in *Laundrette*

> central questions of sexual identity are mixed with discussions of race, economics and generation difference and ... the action constantly swings back and forth between the social and the individual in a manner ... which compels admiration for its vigour and attempt at comprehensiveness.[30]

Hill also noted the rise of a British social art cinema, observing a move among Channel 4-funded films towards a more European style of filmmaking.[31]

Conclusion

This move towards European art cinema correlates with a growing relationship between Britain and Europe in this decade. John Caughie argues that the participation of television in film festivals is a symptom of an emerging 'British art cinema' in the 1970s and 1980s, 'an art cinema, balanced precariously between a European sensibility and the North American market, which is economically dependent on television'.[32] Co-productions were becoming more frequent as government subsidy was scarce and American finance dried up towards the end of the decade.

The channel was also committed to funding international films from an early stage for the Film on Four International strand, and sought co-productions with European companies at festivals like Cannes. Where the channel had sales rights, the European market was crucial in making a return on film investments, as most Films on Four had limited art-house releases and could not hope to recoup in the domestic market. In the 1980s, then, a move towards Europe was taking place, industrially and aesthetically. This chapter has sought to tease out some of the stylistic themes that the partnership between Channel 4 and British film brought to the cinema of the 1980s with the aim of exploring ideas about what the involvement of Channel 4 meant for British cinema beyond the purely industrial determinants of film production.

Notes

1. James Saynor, 'Writer's Television', Sight and Sound, 2 (1992), 30.
2. Anon., 'The Pursuit of Innocents', *Guardian Weekly*, 14 August 1983.
3. Christopher Williams, 'The Social Art Cinema: A Moment in the History of British Film and Television Culture', in *Cinema: The Beginnings and the Future*, ed. by Christopher Williams (London: University of Westminster Press, 1996), 190–200; John Hill, *British Cinema in the 1980s: Issues and Themes* (Oxford: Clarendon Press, 1999); Paul Giles, 'History with Holes: Channel 4 Television Films of the 1980s', in *Fires Were Started: British Cinema and Thatcherism*, ed. by Lester Friedman, 2nd edn (Minneapolis: Minnesota University Press, 1993), 58–74.
4. Samantha Lay, *British Social Realism: From Documentary to Brit-grit* (London: Wallflower Press, 2002).
5. Amy Sargeant, *British Cinema: A Critical History* (London: BFI Publishing, 2005), 300.
6. Michael Coveney, *The World According to Mike Leigh* (London: Harper Collins, 1996), 185.
7. David Rose, personal communication, 27 May 2010.
8. Anon., 'Review: *Another Time Another Place*', *Monthly Film Bulletin* (August 1983), 210–11.
9. Andrew Higson, 'A Green and Pleasant Land: Rural Spaces and British Cinema', in *Representing the Rural: Space, Place and Identity in Films about the Land*, ed. by Catherine Fowler and Gillian Helfield (Detroit: Wayne State University Press, 2006), 240.
10. Annie Morgan James, 'Enchanted Places, Land and Sea, and Wilderness: Scottish Highland Landscape and Identity in Cinema', in *Representing the Rural*, 187.
11. Martin McLoone, 'Landscape in Irish Cinema', in Cinema and Landscape: Film, Nation and Cultural Geography, ed. by Graeme Harper and Jonathan Rayner (Chicago: University of Chicago Press), 140.

12. Steve McIntyre, 'New Images of Scotland', *Screen*, 25:1 (1984), 54.

13. John O'Connor, 'Accounts', *New York Times*, 4 July 1986.

14. Sargeant, *British Cinema*, 318.

15. Paul Kerr, 'The British with their Trousers Down', *The Listener*, 28 August 1986.

16. *Ibid.*

17. Giles, 'History with Holes', 65.

18. *Ibid.*

19. Andrew Higson, 'The Instability of the National', in *British Cinema, Past and Present*, ed. by Higson and Justine Ashby (London: Routledge, 2000), 35–48, 45.

20. Andrew Higson, 'Space, Place, Spectacle', *Screen*, 25: 4–5 (1984), 3.

21. John Hill, 'From the New Wave to Brit Grit: Continuity and Difference in Working-Class Realism', in *British Cinema, Past and Present*, 251.

22. Leonard Quart, 'Review: *Letter to Brezhnev*', *Cineaste*, 15:1 (1986), 48.

23. Barnaby F. Taylor, *The British New Wave* (Manchester: Manchester University Press, 2006), 3.

24. Lay, *British Social Realism*, 95.

25. Larry Coyne, 'TV used to feed off the cinema'.

26. Williams, 'The Social Art Cinema', 193.

27. *Ibid.*

28. John Hill, *Ken Loach: The Politics of Film and Television* (London: BFI, 2011), 168.

29. Williams, 'The Social Art Cinema', 193.

30. *Ibid.*, 199.

31. Hill, 'British Television and Film', in *Big Picture, Small Screen*, 158.

32. John Caughie, 'The Logic of Convergence', in *Big Picture, Small Screen: The Relations Between Film and Television*, ed. by John Hill and Martin McLoone (Luton: University of Luton Press, 1996), 217.

Productive Relationships

Chapter 5

Channel 4's film financing model

Very few opportunities were available to both new and experienced producers in the 1980s. In the early part of the decade, the industry had experienced a boost, with *Chariots of Fire* (Hugh Hudson, 1981) and *Gandhi* (Richard Attenborough, 1982) receiving Academy Awards and Channel 4 and Palace Pictures moving into production. However, by the mid-1980s, this had reversed with the collapse of Goldcrest, the removal of capital allowances and the abolition of the Eady Levy in 1985.[1] By 1990, the film industry had reached a crisis. Overall investment in film declined from £275 million in 1984 to £137 million by 1990. American investment had decreased from £176 million in 1985 to just £67 million by 1988, while 1990 saw the lowest number of films produced in the UK since 1981.[2] At the same time, cinema audiences had increased with the arrival of multiplexes, but cinemagoers were going to see American, not British, films.

In the late 1980s and early 1990s, it became increasingly difficult for new writers, directors and producers to break into the industry. Production costs rose, there was little funding available and there were few sources of government support or tax incentives, and these problems were taking place against the backdrop of a general worldwide recession. By the late 1990s, filmmakers were facing a new set of problems. With the Labour government's support for culture and the arts in Britain and an injection of £100 million from the proceeds of the National Lottery, production rose to almost unprecedented heights, and more filmmakers were making debut features than ever before. However, few producers made money on their first films, and it was difficult to raise development money for second features. Production increased, but the old problems associated with distribution remained. The advent of lottery funding in 1995 led to a spike in production (at its peak, 128 films were produced in 1996) but many of these films did not find distribution. In the 1990s, of the 966 films that the British Film Institute identifies as being British, 317 were never released.[3] This had not changed by the latter part of the decade. In 1997, Labour

Table 5.1 British films produced 1980–1999

Year	Films produced	Channel 4 productions	Year	Films produced	Channel 4 productions
1980	58	–	1990	51	15
1981	40	–	1991	59	23
1982	67	14	1992	47	17
1983	37	18	1993	67	12
1984	70	16	1994	84	15
1985	58	22	1995	78	19
1986	56	11	1996	128	14
1987	72	21	1997	116	18
1988	60	23	1998	88	16
1989	45	12	1999	100	33

Sources: BFI, John Pym, *Film on Four: A Survey* (London: BFI, 1992), *Screen Finance*.

announced a strategy to assist in the development of the industry, and commissioned the Film Policy Group to propose a number of structural and economic measures to implement this. The group found the main problem with the industry to be that it continued to be fragmented and production-led.[4]

Being a film producer in the 1980s and 1990s

Many filmmakers did not have access to distribution or to exhibition on the major circuits, as these were largely dominated by the US majors. Furthermore, there was also the longstanding problem of the gap between production and distribution: American studios controlled major distribution circuits, and it was extremely difficult to achieve a wide release with independent exhibitors, which meant that many films went into production without the guarantee of UK distribution. The industry was unsustainable, particularly for smaller companies which came into existence for the life of a film and then disbanded when the production was finished.[5] Indeed, in the 1980s, 454 films were produced by 342 companies.[6] As Sarah Street stated, 'companies come and go, and with them ideas and styles which, in a more stable economic environment, might have been developed in subsequent films'.[7]

For an independent producer without the support of a major studio, finding finance in the UK was a difficult and complex process. Producers might receive equity investment (i.e. money the investors could expect to recoup through profit) from one or more sources; for example, in the case of *The Crying Game* (Neil Jordan, 1992) this was Channel 4 and British Screen. Producers would then try to offset more of the budget by selling distribution rights to foreign territories such as Europe and North America, while they could also potentially sell the television rights for a further 10–20% of the budget. The funding process itself was very complicated. The producer had to marshal funds from a variety of disparate sources as there was very little money available, and this funding was almost always linked to European sources and North American distribution rights. Indeed, the producer became central to the film-funding process for this reason. Producers worked tirelessly to provide the creative space for a production, attempting to draw together complex contracts in a way that would placate the interests of all investors. The producer was therefore crucial to the success of the film.

Producers could secure funding through five main avenues. Perhaps the most common method of financing was from broadcasters such as Channel 4 or the BBC. Broadcasters would seldom fund a film fully, so this finance was usually used in conjunction with backing from a variety of other sources. Filmmakers could apply for funding through government initiatives (the Arts Council of Great Britain, Regional Arts Associations, the Scottish Arts Council, the Scottish Film Council, the Welsh Arts Council, the Welsh Films Board, British Screen and the National Film Development Fund). However, many of these associations asked for submissions by artists or concerning the arts, and the National Film Boards tended to stipulate residency in their specific regions as a condition for funding. Aside from British Screen (a semi-commercial organisation which received £1.5 million per year), state funding for producers was extremely limited.[8] Producers could also seek sponsorship from the BFI Production Board, which could grant up to £300,000 for low-budget, non-commercial features. The BFI had a firm cultural policy to support artists, and throughout the 1980s and 1990s it supported filmmakers such as Peter Greenaway, Derek Jarman and Terence Davies. Bank finance or commercial finance from city institutions was also an option (though a rarity at a time when the industry was in decline). More commonly, producers would 'pre-sell' the territorial rights of their films to distributors, obtaining an agreement for the distributors to pay out on completion of the film. This could then be taken to a bank to obtain a loan against the guarantee. Producers could also seek co-production partners in other independent film companies (such as Rediffusion Films).

Channel 4's film financing model

Amid these disparate funding forms, Channel 4 was able to offer substantial support to filmmakers; support which was, crucially, not predicated on artistic, stylistic or residential conditions. In theory, the only concerns faced by filmmakers when working with the channel related to budgetary limitations and the personal taste of the Commissioning Editors. Channel 4 tended to offer three main types of financial deal to independent producers, and these are detailed as follows:

1. Full funding: On rare occasions, the channel would fully fund a production (in 1984, this could be anywhere up to around £500,000, rising to around £1.8 million in 1997). This was the case with Stephen Frears's *My Beautiful Laundrette* and Danny Boyle's *Trainspotting* (1996).
2. Co-funding: The channel could also (more commonly) enter into co-production deals with other producers. In this case they would usually offer equity investment in the production, as well as buying the television rights (at a cost of around £300,000). This was the method of financing employed with *The Crying Game*, *Four Weddings and a Funeral* (Mike Newell, 1994) and *The Neon Bible* (Terence Davies, 1995).
3. Broadcast rights only: Lastly, the channel could simply pre-buy the television rights to a production, offering no equity investment but gaining the right to broadcast it a number of times.

Buying television rights while a film was still in production meant that the channel was still investing in the film (it was thus 'Channel 4-funded' and could be referred to as such), and this also meant that the channel owned the sole rights to the UK television premiere. This type of funding can be seen in *A Room with a View*, Neil Jordan's *Mona Lisa* (1986) and Shekhar Kapur's *Elizabeth* (1998). In this way, the channel could provide money for larger-budget productions and screen them on television with little risk involved.[9] However, Channel 4 also blurred the lines between co-financing and television rights, as the Drama Department would sometimes still seek creative and editorial input on productions where it had no investment but had simply bought the right to broadcast. It could also offer further money on an ad-hoc basis throughout the course of a production, to plug gaps in City financing.[10] Thus, while the funding packages outlined above were the general rule, the channel was also able to operate with a certain amount of flexibility.

These funding packages remained largely the same throughout the life of Film on Four. However, whereas David Rose would fund around twenty films per year, David Aukin preferred to put more money into fewer films (around twelve to fifteen per year). For Aukin, fewer films on Film on Four's yearly slate meant that the channel could secure larger equity investments in bigger-budget co-productions. This involved taking more risk, but it also meant that the channel would be in a better position to recoup its investment and would also gain greater creative and editorial input. According to Aukin:

> there is an optimum number of films we can get involved in editorially. The answer is not to make lots more pictures. We will take more TV rights in more films and over time commission more and take more rights, in order to increase our percentage of involvement in films.[11]

Aukin's department continued to buy television rights, and also to fully fund those productions that were considered to be less than commercial (such as the films of Ken Loach and Mike Leigh). However, fully funded productions became rarer after the mid-1980s as production costs rose considerably.

Independent companies

Generally speaking, there were three different types of independent company supplying a variety of programming (not just feature films) to Channel 4 throughout the 1980s and early 1990s: small companies with a turnover of under £500,000 per year (the so-called 'man, dog and answerphone'); medium-sized companies with a turnover of up to £2 million; and large, fully capitalised companies like Carlton and Zenith, which differed little in structure and profit from the main ITV companies, aside from the right to broadcast terrestrially.[12] In terms of film production, these varied from the small companies set up to make one film; the medium-sized companies which had achieved a significant catalogue of films but which could go bust at any time with just one flop (this described the situation faced by Working Title throughout the 1980s); and the larger companies with varied commercial interests and/ or longstanding deals with American studios (this could describe what Working Title eventually became, or how Palace Pictures stood financially in the late 1980s). The following case study of the small independent company Partners in Production (responsible for the early Film on Four *Accounts* [Michael Darlow, 1982]) will chart the creation and consolidation of the new and burgeoning independent sector in the early 1980s, exploring an important historical turning point in the British film and television industries – the creation of the independent sector following the arrival of Channel 4 – and discussing what this new opportunity meant to filmmakers working in the industry.

The arrival of Channel 4 in 1982 effectively created the independent sector. In the 1970s, during the campaign for the fourth channel, groups such as the Association of Independent Producers (AIP) had utilised Thatcherite rhetoric, painting the independents as small businessmen struggling to break free of the monolithic duopoly of the BBC and ITV in the name of free-market competition.[13] It was a campaign which worked well. In his speech at the Edinburgh Film Festival in 1979, Jeremy Isaacs had proposed that independents should provide 10% of the channel's broadcasting output. However, by the time the channel went on air, independents had come to supply around 50% of its programming (the other 50% being provided by the ITV companies and American imports). This was a significant victory, as, in 1979, independent productions had formed just 1% of broadcasting output.[14] Sylvia Harvey argues that the 1980s were marked by a tension between the old and new right; one stood for heritage and the preservation of old traditions, and the other for trade and free-market enterprise. This tension is especially evident in the 1980 Broadcasting Act which created Channel 4. The remit to 'innovate' hailed from longstanding public service traditions, while the idea of the 'publishing house' created a highly competitive market where freelancing and impermanent employment was the norm.[15]

Within a few years, over 1,000 independent companies had sprung up to provide programming for the channel. By the late 1980s and early 1990s, independents were also providing programming for the ITV and the BBC following the 25% rule proposed in 1986, which stipulated that both broadcasters must outsource 25% of their airtime to independent producers by 1992.[16] While the BBC and ITV still employed in-house staff, many new small, medium and larger companies were created, with many brought into existence for the purposes of just one production.[17] Jeremy Isaacs and the channel's Managing Director Justin Dukes had wanted to create a sector that had a limited ability to grow, which would in theory ensure that the channel did not become too reliant on a few large companies (which might begin to work against its interests).[18] However, there were significant problems with this model. The independent sector was highly competitive, with a large number of companies producing programmes but not necessarily receiving repeat commissions, as the channel was under no obligation to work with such companies again.[19] The sector was heavily dependent on the channel, and many small companies struggled to survive as a result.[20] Many programme makers also saw the competitive nature of this free-market model as exploitative, as there is a tendency for any free market to become dominated by large companies, which push out the smaller, less efficient companies.[21] However, Martyn Auty argues that, although not without its problems, the channel ultimately worked to the benefit of programme makers operating in the independent sector, a sector which was

> once a wilderness of grant-aided filmmakers, [and] is now a flourishing garden, ploughed and tended by producers who either dropped out of establishment TV to find greater freedom of expression, or dragged themselves belatedly out of the dwindling counter-culture to make mainstream programmes for mass audiences.[22]

The publishing ethos of Channel 4 meant that over 4,000 jobs were created in London alone, heralding a massive boost in employment and opportunities for previously marginalised programme makers to be heard.[23]

With the Film on Four strand, the channel offered opportunities to independent filmmakers to produce low-budget films in an environment which prioritised creative freedom and cultural imperatives over profit. David Rose sought to provide a training ground for new talent, while many first-time writers and directors would also benefit from the kudos associated with working on films for theatrical release. In the channel's early days, many producers found an atmosphere that was conducive to creativity with few editorial impositions. However, the relationship between the

Fiction Department and independent filmmakers was also fraught with tension as the channel struggled to find its feet with the commissioning process. Some producers argued that they suffered incompetence, broken deals and mismanagement at the hands of Commissioning Editors, many of whom had little experience working in the film industry (David Rose had come from a television background, while script editors Karin Bamborough and Walter Donohue had theatre backgrounds).[24] As a result, the AIP accused the administrative systems of being 'weak'.[25] John Ellis, who produced *Visions*, a series of fifteen programmes about world cinema, talks about how the relationship between the channel and independents changed in 1983 following the first round of commissions:

> The channel came to negotiate the second phase of its relationship with the companies that it had brought into being. At this point, the implicit model altered. Instead of the arts funding body and client relationship, there emerged the more traditional relationship between the freelance employee and the institutional employer. Companies were kept waiting until the last possible moment for news about whether their commission would be renewed; renewals were for six or seven months rather than for a year; competition for some commissions emerged between both new and established groups; and some of the production companies were brought up against their nature as capitalist enterprises rather than as collective endeavours.[26]

Producers also complained about access to Commissioning Editors, arguing that it took months for them to receive a decision on their submissions, while all the while they suspended projects just in case the channel gave them the green light. They argued that their scripts were not evaluated properly because of the sheer volume of submissions, lack of staff to deal with them and few criteria on which to judge them.[27] Problems arose regarding how thorough the evaluating process was for filmmakers submitting scripts without the backing of a major company. Theoretically anyone could submit a script, though this was not always the case. First-time producers were often infuriated by dismissals or advice that they should take their proposals to larger production companies and approach the channel that way.[28]

Simon Perry, producer of *Another Time, Another Place* (1983), saw this first year as a learning process for both the independents and Commissioning Editors, concluding that both filmmakers and Channel 4 learned much from the experience, as well as having to adjust their expectations:

> Some film-makers have been expecting Channel 4 to behave like
> a milk cow, doling out funds like a grant-aiding body, rather than
> seeing it for what it is – a professional, commercially minded
> enterprise. Channel 4 remains the best thing that has happened to
> the British film industry.[29]

During this period, the channel was acquainting itself with the independent sector – those commissioning programmes had never had to deal with producers before, and the administrative structures in place were new and untested.[30] But despite these initial problems, in 1984 David Rose stated that 'the independent sector is alive and kicking and the submissions are likewise. It's almost a miracle, the things we've achieved over the last eighteen months'.[31]

Through Film on Four, many of the small independents hoping to produce programming for the channel gained the opportunity to move into feature-film production. Partners in Production was a small company which also functioned as a collective in which the members were all equal shareholders. It comprised thirty-six writers, directors and technicians who also simultaneously freelanced for other companies. Tom Sachs, producer of *Accounts*, stated that this was because the company wanted to avoid becoming too dependent on Channel 4 for finance, and was looking into other sources of finance for projects in addition to the channel.[32] The group was thus set up to offer its practitioners work yet maintain their freedom to work elsewhere.[33] *Accounts* was fully funded by Channel 4 and was commissioned in the first batch of Films on Four. Originally a stage play, its author Michael Wilcox, a member of the company, developed the script with Channel 4 after being approached by Walter Donohue, who had suggested to David Rose that the play be made into a film.

Accounts follows Mary Mawson, a widow who moves with her two sons to Northumbria to manage a farm after the death of her husband. The film is a celebration of regionalism, and gives an extremely realistic portrayal of the day-to-day trials of running a farm. This serves as a backdrop to a storyline which explores the emotional fallout when Mary's youngest son is revealed to be homosexual. The film itself stands as an example of the experimental nature of the early days of Channel 4. John O'Connor of the *New York Times* stated that *Accounts* provided an 'almost cinema verite [sic] glimpse of day-to-day life in a contemporary rural setting'.[34] Director Michael Darlow was aiming for a naturalist aesthetic, using first-time actors and allowing them time to get used to farming processes well in advance of filming. The narrative is by no means fast-paced, and the film makes few concessions to the narrative conventions of cinema. In his 1991 filmography of Channel 4 films John Pym describes *Accounts* as 'a small film, happily embracing its regionalism'. Life on the Mawson farm simply unfolds almost as though the viewer were a fly on the wall, at times to uncomfortable effect, as it can feel as though the viewer is intruding into the Mawsons' domestic life and personal dramas. Location shots consistently evoke a deep connection between the family and the landscape they inhabit. This is juxtaposed with the cramped, domestic setting of the Mawsons' living room, resulting in a deeply intimate and personal film. *Accounts* was to be released in a cinema in Piccadilly Circus, but when the cinema closed down the film was instead broadcast in the first ever Film on Four season. It was, however, later shown on the American Public Broadcasting Service as part of a retrospective season of Films on Four in 1986.[35]

What was unusual for Darlow (who had been heavily involved in the campaign for the fourth channel) was the amount of technical and creative freedom that the crew enjoyed on the production. The casting and shooting of the film were somewhat unconventional. The crew wanted to cast untrained actors, a creative decision which Channel 4 backed because, according to Darlow, the channel was in principle very much against using stars.[36] With the aim of portraying an accurate sense of agricultural life, the two boys lived on the farm for three months before shooting, learning the script as well as a variety of farming methods. Furthermore, although David Rose and Walter Donohue were briefed on the progress of the production, there were few editorial or creative constraints. There was a cost controller on set who monitored the production, but did not interfere.[37] Darlow, who had worked for years within the company structures of the BBC and ITV, described his experience working on *Accounts* as 'liberating', because although 'it wasn't that one's work with the BBC and Thames weren't good [sic] ... it was much more regimented'.[38]

This had much to do with less restrictive practices. Big production companies (with the exception of Goldcrest) were actually unsuited to working with Channel 4, because of their high overheads and restrictive union practices.[39] The channel worked best with production companies that could deal with its weekly system of cost-control management.[40] In order to function efficiently the channel needed a less conventional way of operating, without the interference of unions such as the ACTT. To facilitate this, terms of trade were agreed between the channel and the

Independent Programme Producers Association (IPPA), a company set up to represent the interests of the new independent companies. As part of these terms, the IPPA adopted the Short Films Agreement, which was traditionally used to allow short corporate films to be made with reduced crew and lower budgets.[41] However, the agreement applied only to those films which were fully funded by the channel; co-productions tended to be governed by their own unique rules.[42]

Methods of funding and rights issues as set out in the terms of trade soon became a subject of concern for the IPPA. Where the channel would fully fund a programme, it would allocate producers a production fee in addition to the budget, ensuring that the producers were paid. But the channel also kept the rights to the programme, and if it made a profit, the channel would split this 70/30 with the programme makers. However, Michael Darlow argued that although this presented problems for some more commercially minded companies, many producers were unconcerned with the monetary aspects and were enjoying the freedom to make programmes in a way that they never had before:

> there was a feeling amongst the more commercial producers that they should have more of it, but then they were more willing to risk more of the money. But to most of us . . who were coming in, we just wanted to make the programmes we wanted to make the way we wanted to make them. That's what motivated us … But essentially we were interested in creativity, alternative voices … it wasn't about the commerce.[43]

Indeed, realising that budgets were a concern for the channel, producers were willing to work for less in the early days because they had an ideological investment in the channel and wanted to ensure its survival.

Film on Four, operating within the channel's wider remit for 'innovation', offered independents a new outlet for creativity, with fewer ideological, technical and commercial constraints. David Rose believed that his department should be

> supporting films that would never see the light of day in the commercial sector. I don't know whether *The Ploughman's Lunch* or *Another Time, Another Place* would have been supported commercially but we've got to hang on to what we believe to be quality indigenous films – the kind of film that financiers don't jump up and down about.[44]

Indeed, *Accounts* is a good example of the type of film that Rose and his department set out to commission. It was the kind of film which might not have been made without Channel 4 funding, dealing as it did with themes of homosexuality as well as placing an unusual focus on the mundane agrarian specificities of British culture. This was something that John O'Connor also noted in his review of the PBS Film on Four season:

> The one common denominator of these productions is an unblinking exploration of segments of British society that tend to be neglected in dizzy comedies or costume dramas. They deal with aspects of contemporary Britain not found in the tourist brochures.[45]

Producer Simon Perry also recognised Channel 4's contribution to British film culture through the funding of such productions: 'The mid 1970's were really drab, a real dead zone for movies of a genuinely British character. Now that's changed. The output of modest budget films has improved dramatically, mainly due to Channel 4.'[46] Indeed, the channel was often the first port of call for new producers seeking co-production finance, and it even served as something of a training ground – with its strict budgets and highly efficient cost-control processes, the channel shaped the expectations of producers and directors, effectively offering many new filmmakers a useful education in production.[47]

But there were those who criticised this method of funding. In 1990 independent producer Don Boyd, a vocal critic of Film on Four, argued that in working with producers the channel

> served its own needs, to great critical acclaim . . . Channel 4 has often thrived at the expense of those who wanted to make films, relying on them to raise money. And there have been no big hits on Film on Four of the scale of *Diva* or *Sex, Lies and Videotape*.[48]

Some producers also found negotiations with the channel frustrating, but were bound by a lack of choice. Charles Gormley, director of *Living Apart Together* (1983), described his relationship with the channel as 'slightly uncomfortable . . . but it's the only partnership available to you unless you can hack it with an American major and that's murder'.[49] Other independents were grateful for a much-needed source of additional finance. For example, Lezli-An Barrett, director of the Channel 4/ Cannon-funded film *Business as Usual* (1988), stated that without the co-financing support of Channel 4 her film almost certainly would not have been made.[50] Brian Gilbert, director of *Runners* (1983), also argued that the channel provided some continuity of funding at a time of few opportunities:

> At present each film-maker feels like a hitchhiker. Each thinks it's a miracle to get a lift. But in fact, quite a few *are* getting lifts. 'Film on Four' guarantees the opportunity to make films, which is the only way we'll see anything new emerging. But don't start looking for a collective vision at this stage.[51]

The channel's support also carried a lot of weight with potential co-producers. According to Colin McCabe, once producers had secured Channel 4 backing, it was 'very easy to raise the rest. Often it is just a matter of finding a distributor in the states. Even if the film fails in cinemas he [sic] knows he will be able to recover his costs from home box office'.[52]

However, it is important to remember that although the channel offered some measure of continuity to filmmakers, it did not offer sustainability. It says much about the state of filmmaking in Britain that the entire industry was swayed by this tiny source of finance. In the midst of a period of severe decline, Channel 4 had, unintentionally, come to form the backbone of British filmmaking, and it was this fact that caused Nick Medley to state in 1990 that '[t]he 1980s effectively saw the film industry starved, beaten senseless and plugged into a life support system called Channel 4'.[53] For many, Channel 4 became the banner of the new film industry,[54] despite the fact that the amount of money that the channel offered each year (around £6 million in 1982, rising to just £11 million in 1991) was a drop in the ocean. Indeed, though the annual budget of Film on Four went towards funding some twenty films yearly, in Hollywood this sum would have been the equivalent of one low-budget production. The problem was, of course, a lack of sustainability in the industry – many companies just did not have the finance necessary to develop a 'slate' of films, whereby a few successes could absorb a multitude of failures. Even big companies like Goldcrest had gone bust for this reason.

Conclusion

The advent of Channel 4, with its limited finances, did little to change the state of filmmaking in Britain. But throughout the 1980s and 1990s, the channel did provide a much-needed source of finance for low-budget features, and in many cases fully funded films which might otherwise have had difficulty in attracting financiers. The channel also offered co-production finance to producers forced to seek funding from a variety of sources, and indeed, as filmmaking costs rose considerably throughout the decade, the co-production became the channel's most common form of sponsorship. For many producers seeking co-finance, the channel was often the first port of call, and its involvement in a production could also attract other investors. Importantly, as the case of *Accounts* shows, Channel 4 also came to offer a cultural outlet for filmmakers: a chance to make films free from commercial constraints, and films which dealt with traditionally non-commercial subjects.

Notes

1. House of Commons, National Heritage Committee, 'The British Film Industry' (London: 1995).
2. Nick Medley and John Woodward, *Productive Relationships?* (London: BFI, 1991), vii.
3. Phil Wickham, *Producing the Goods? UK Film Production, 1991–2001* (London: BFI, 2002), 3.
4. Deloitte and Touche, *The Cost of Making Dreams: Accounting for the British Film Industry* (London: BFI, 1999).
5. *Ibid.*, 47.
6. Richard Paterson, 'Changing Conditions of Independent Production in the UK' in *New Questions of British Cinema*, ed. by Duncan Petrie (London: BFI Publishing, 1991), 48.
7. Sarah Street, *British National Cinema* (Oxford: Taylor and Francis, 1997), 110.
8. Amanda Harcourt, *The Independent Producer: Film and Television* (London: Faber & Faber, 1986), 109.
9. BFI Special Collections, Papers of Roger Graef, CF Paper 312, 'Film on Four' (1985).
10. Harcourt, *The Independent Producer*, 129.
11. *Screen International*, 9 September 1997.
12. Paterson, 'Changing Conditions', 48.
13. Ian Potter, *The Rise and Rise of Independents* (Isleworth: Guerilla Books, 2008), 80.
14. *Ibid.*, 82.
15. Sylvia Harvey, 'Channel 4 Television: From Annan to Grade', in *Behind the Screens: The Structure of British Television in the Nineties*, ed. by Stuart Hood (London: Lawrence & Wishart, 1999), 102–32, 103.
16. Colin Spark, 'Independent Production, Unions, and Casualisation', in *Behind the Screens*, 136.
17. *Ibid.*, 136.
18. John Woodward, 'Organising for Change', in *The Broadcasting Debate 1*, ed. by Richard Paterson (London: BFI Publishing, 1990), 83.

19. Anon., 'Jeremy Isaacs Reports Back', *AIP&Co*, 48 (1983), 4–5.
20. *Ibid.*
21. Spark, 'Independent Production', in *Behind the Screens*, 143.
22. Anon., 'A Year of Living Differently', *Time Out*, 27 November 1983.
23. *Ibid.*
24. *Ibid.*
25. *Ibid.*
26. John Ellis, 'Channel 4: Working Notes', *Screen*, 24:6 (1983), 40.
27. *Ibid.*
28. *Ibid.*
29. *Ibid.*
30. Anthony Hayward, 'Producers at Loggerheads over Films on Four', *Screen International*, 11 June 1983.
31. Anon., *AIP & CO*, 52 (March 1984), 27.
32. Michael Darlow, personal communication, 9 December 2011.
33. Anon., 'Darlow Film on Four for next season', *Stage* (July 1983), 19.
34. John O'Connor, 'Accounts', *New York Times*, 4 July 1986.
35. Michael Darlow, personal communication, 9 December 2011.
36. *Ibid.*
37. *Ibid.*
38. *Ibid.*
39. Paul Bonner with Leslie Aston, *Independent Television in Britain Volume 6: New Developments in Independent Television* (Basingstoke: Palgrave, 2003), 198.
40. *Ibid.*
41. Potter, *The Rise and Rise of Independents*, 85.
42. Harcourt, *The Independent Producer*, 111.
43. Michael Darlow, personal communication, 9 December 2011.
44. Anon., *AIP & CO*, 52 (March 1984), 24.
45. O'Connor, 'Accounts', *New York Times*, 4 July 1986.
46. *City Limits*, 15 July 1983.
47. Harcourt, *The Independent Producer*, 110.
48. Nicholas Fraser, 'Small No Longer Beautiful on 4', *The Observer*, 4 February 1990.
49. Duncan Petrie, *Creativity and Constraint in the British Film Industry* (London: Palgrave, 1991), 84.
50. *Television Today*, 4 June 1987.
51. *4 This Month* (May 1984), 3.
52. *Sunday Times*, 21 February 1988.
53. Woodward, *Productive Relationships?*, 1.
54. *The Observer*, 4 February 1990.

Chapter 6

A tale of two film companies

Case studies of two film companies that Channel 4 worked with regularly, Palace and Working Title, form the spine of this chapter, which aims to explore the channel's editorial and creative relationships with independent companies, its editorial decision-making processes and its priorities towards the filmmakers it sponsored. Palace was an independent company with interests not just in film production but also in theatrical and video distribution, post-production and exhibition. The company received support from Channel 4 on many of their projects, including *The Company of Wolves* (Neil Jordan, 1984), *Letter to Brezhnev* (Chris Bernard, 1985), *Mona Lisa* (Jordan, 1986) and *The Crying Game* (Neil Jordan, 1992). However, with the exception of *The Crying Game*, these productions would arguably have been successful without the channel's support (though the channel was instrumental in developing the script for *The Company of Wolves*). Working Title began as a small independent company which formed in the early 1980s and grew rapidly to become one of the most successful production companies in Britain, bringing considerable economic and critical success to the industry through productions such as *My Beautiful Laundrette* (Stephen Frears, 1985), *Four Weddings and a Funeral* (Mike Newell, 1994) and *Notting Hill* (Roger Michell, 1999).

Palace Pictures

Palace was set up by Nik Powell in the early 1980s following his long career at Virgin with co-partner Richard Branson. It was Branson's business model that Powell attempted to emulate when he sold his shares to Virgin in the late 1970s and attempted to set up his own company. Palace began with a video store, and soon launched its own video label (much in the same way as Virgin had launched its music label following its chain of music stores). Part of Powell's severance deal with Virgin included a stake in the Scala Cinema, as well as ownership of a post-production video editing facility, meaning that Palace was able to develop interests in post-production and exhibition as well as video distribution.[1] It was during the early days of the company that Powell saw potential in Stephen Woolley, a Palace employee who was then running the Scala, screening programmes of niche, art-house films while managing to turn a decent profit. Woolley's passion for cinema coupled with Powell's financial skills made for a very productive relationship, and Woolley was soon offered a 50% stake in the company. At Woolley's instigation, Palace quickly moved into theatrical as well as video distribution, buying the rights to both Sam Raimi's *The Evil Dead* (1981) and Jean-Jacques Beineix's *Diva* (1981). Woolley and Powell added a personal dimension to film buying, and would fly all over the world to convince producers that they were passionate about their films and would do them justice as distributors.[2] The company grew steadily until 1983, but soon faced problems as they began to find themselves outbid on distribution deals by richer rivals, and also by smaller companies that sought to emulate their buying practices. The answer for Palace seemed to lie in production, as the company would then own the rights to the films it produced and could sell their distribution rights abroad as well as build up a library of titles. As a result, Palace had something which was rare among independent companies in the 1980s: the ability to distribute its own productions. By the time the company went bust in 1992, it had produced a total of nineteen films.[3]

Palace moved into production in 1984, and the company's style was very much determined by its image, which by this time was well established. Palace tended to acquire specialist independent films that would have been difficult to access elsewhere, films which went against the grain of literary realism and often dealt with controversial themes and taboo issues (*The Company of Wolves, Dust Devil* [Richard Stanley, 1992]), threats to the political establishment (*Scandal* [Michael Caton-Jones, 1989]) and provocative social and sexual themes (*Mona Lisa, The Crying Game*). Like Working Title, the company's films concentrated on local stories, but in a way that appealed to international audiences, and it was one of the only independents able to attract both niche and larger cross-over audiences.[4] Palace gained a reputation in the industry for producing innovative projects and for acquiring and distributing films which gained a cult following. Palace's distribution arm was its main strength, and as Phil Wickham argues, many of the films the company released would come to 'define the decade for British cinema'.[5] However, while the company's productivity in production and distribution was admired, Palace frequently drew criticism regarding its haphazard management style, and many industry figures deeply resented what they saw as the company's 'happy go arrogant' approach.[6] One Palace collaborator stated that 'critics saw Nik and Steve as wide boys who were flogging brown nylon shirts off the back of a truck somewhere in Chapel Street market. They just didn't see them as legitimate traders.'[7] This was an image that Palace both tried to perpetuate and also struggled to overcome.

While Powell was considered to be a 'money man', dealing with all aspects of the business, Woolley was passionate about cinema and tended to see himself as a filmmaker rather than a producer, sharing a close creative relationship with directors, particularly Neil Jordan, and continually emphasising the cultural value of the films that he wanted to make. The company distributed forty-six films throughout the 1980s and early 1990s, eleven of which were co-produced or sponsored by Channel 4. The first Channel 4 film that Palace released theatrically was *Angel* (Neil Jordan, 1982). Woolley first saw the film at Cannes and was so impressed with its poetic visual storytelling that he was determined to acquire it for UK theatrical release, which meant negotiating with the channel.[8] Channel 4 was initially wary of giving the film a theatrical release as the channel had it earmarked for television, but without this Palace would have been unable to release it on video.[9] After some weeks of negotiation with Larry Coyne of Film Four International, a compromise was reached and the film was exhibited in the Scala Cinema for two weeks.[10] *Angel*, crucially, also saw the genesis of Stephen Woolley's long creative relationship with writer and director Neil Jordan. The types of films that Channel 4 sponsored were thus of interest to Palace, and though the company did not directly benefit from the channel's funding practices until the mid-1980s, it did share in some of the channel's early successes through the distribution side of the company.[11]

Palace's relationship with Channel 4 has been described as 'extraordinarily fruitful' though 'sometimes edgy',[12] and this certainly characterised many of their collaborations. The first film Palace produced with Channel 4 funding was *The Company of Wolves*. The novelist Angela Carter had been commissioned by the channel to write a 30-minute script based on her short story 'The Company of Wolves', which had been a radio play. Neil Jordan read the script but felt that it needed to be longer. He brought it to the attention of Woolley, who approached David Rose and the National Film Development Fund and managed to raise enough money to turn it into a feature-length screenplay.[13] Carter and Jordan fleshed out the script, a gothic fantasy loosely based on the story of Little Red Riding Hood, with most of the narrative taking place within the dream of a young girl just reaching puberty. The script was loaded with potent sexual imagery and special effects which would have been very difficult to achieve. According to Woolley, when David Rose and Walter Donohue read the finished article, they 'really didn't like it' as it 'all seemed to them to be too bloody and gory'.[14] Woolley felt that the genre elements of the film did not sit well with Rose and Donohue's initial hopes for the project.[15] In the end it was Lew Grade's company ITC which took a chance on the film, although Channel 4 later acquired it for the Film on Four slot, paying around £300,000 for the television rights. At the time of its release the film was not well received, but it soon achieved cult status and became recognised as a radical, innovative departure for British cinema during an era which dealt predominantly with naturalism and contemporary social concerns.

Palace had also received financing from the channel to produce Chris Bernard's *Letter to Brezhnev*, a socio-political romance set in the drab streets of writer Frank Clarke's hometown of Kirkby in Liverpool. Clarke had originally written the film as a play and had tried for many years to secure funding to develop it into a feature film. After many fruitless attempts, Clarke and Bernard managed to raise £50,000 from local sources to shoot a rough cut, reasoning that they might be able to gain more interest by screening their work to potential financiers.[16] Eventually, Palace stepped in and brought *Brezhnev* to the attention of Karin Bamborough, offering guaranteed distribution for the film if Channel 4 would provide the extra finance needed to complete it.[17] *Brezhnev* was released to critical acclaim, later securing viewing figures of over five million for the channel. However, despite the success of *Letter to Brezhnev*, the relationship between Channel 4 and Palace continued to be fraught with disagreements.

Rejection was something that Woolley was to subsequently experience when attempting to raise finance for the production of *Mona Lisa*. Channel 4 was one of the many companies that rejected the script on the grounds of themes of drug use and prostitution, though the Channel later bought it for television after it was completed. On broadcast it attracted 7.8 million viewers, a record for the channel.[13] According to Woolley, the problem was one of delayed commitment:

> [Aukin would say] 'OK I can see that you have got something here and I'll reluctantly back it, very reluctantly back it.' And I think that

> was the thing that we didn't have with David Rose. David Rose didn't reluctantly back *Company of the Wolves* and he didn't reluctantly back *Mona Lisa*, he *belatedly* backed them. Difference. Big difference, when you're at the sharp end of a movie as a film producer, and you need that money … because you sit there in meetings with loads of lawyers, and they don't want to hear about what you *think* you're going to get for the film.[19]

For Woolley, the key difference in terms of working with David Aukin was that, although Aukin tended to become more involved editorially (particularly at the script stage), this involvement culminated in a creative as well as financial investment in a project.

Regarding *Letter to Brezhnev*, Woolley stated that the co-production was 'one of the best partnerships we ever had' and that it particularly highlighted the extent to which Channel 4 and Palace 'were more than well suited to working together.'[20] On the surface, Film on Four would seem to share some of Palace's core values, particularly in the company's commitment to training new talent and its remit to fund innovative productions that might not otherwise attract finance. Furthermore, though David Rose tended not to be prescriptive about what made a good 'Film on Four', originality and innovation undoubtedly formed part of his criteria. He stated that scripts should be 'fresh and unfamiliar . . . I want to be surprised. I don't want, over the first 10 pages, to feel that I've been there before and that it's derivative.'[21] When asked if Palace had any specific cultural remit in terms of the films it produced, Nik Powell stated: 'Not really. We try to develop new talent, and our films as a result tend to be innovative and interesting. But I have to say that interesting and innovative films tend to score better with the punters as well.'[22] Despite having no established cultural objectives, Palace had, by the late 1980s, gained a reputation for supporting new talent and for taking a chance on subjects that were riskier than those with which more commercially minded producers were perhaps willing to engage. Indeed, Paul Webster, who took over FilmFour in 1998, had gained much of his experience in film distribution working for Palace in the early 1980s.

However, it is possible to note certain stylistic tendencies in Channel 4 films which might go some way towards explaining this reluctance. For example, Rose tended to favour naturalism over non-naturalism (partly because of budgetary concerns) and prioritised the contemporary subject over the historical film or adaptation.[23] According to James Saynor, Rose's 'cinema' prioritised the writer rather than the director, and this was perhaps influenced by Rose's time as a producer of single plays and serials at BBC Pebble Mill prior to his move to the channel.[24] On the other hand, Woolley had always been interested in the visual and the more aesthetically thrilling aspects of cinema across a wide range of genres and cultures. Indeed, the introduction of genre elements into the script for *Company of Wolves* seemed to cause Rose and Donohue apprehension.

Aside from *Company* and *Mona Lisa*, which are considered part of the Film on Four catalogue by virtue of the fact that the channel pre-purchased the television rights to these productions, genre films that drew upon established American cinematic styles were uncommon among the Films on Four of the 1980s. Though the films of Peter Greenaway, Derek Jarman and Terence Davies were visually experimental and followed non-naturalist aesthetics, these productions tend to fit more comfortably into the category of 'art-house' cinema and were the result of numerous ongoing collaborations between Channel 4 and the BFI throughout this decade. What this highlights is that although Channel 4 was far less restricted than the BBC in terms of production practices and their PSB remit, there was nevertheless a tension between producers like Powell and Woolley and the stories they wanted to tell, and the interests of a sponsor like Channel 4. In the case of Working Title, the company's creative interests were often closely aligned with those of Film on Four, and *My Beautiful Laundrette* in many ways came to represent the typical 'Channel 4 production' as much as it did the 'Working Title film'. Working Title also worked well with the channel financially, and is cited by Paul Bonner and Leslie Aston as being one of the aforementioned production companies which dealt well with Channel 4's financial management processes.[25] Palace, as we shall see, tended to suffer from financial setbacks and mismanagement on many of its productions.

The creative interests of Palace and Channel 4 aligned in 1991 with the production of Richard Stanley's *Dust Devil. Dust Devil* is a supernatural fantasy horror about a demonic creature that poses as a hitchhiker and preys on lonely drifters. Set on the arid plains of Namibia, it tells the story of Wendy, a young woman fleeing her abusive husband. As she drives aimlessly into the desert, she is followed by a mysterious American hitchhiker (the demonic 'Dust Devil') who at times seems more ghost than human. The two begin a relationship which the demon is reluctant to end in his customarily violent way because he finds himself growing attached to his prey. *Dust Devil* is a confusing mix of western and European styles and genres, drawing many influences from cinema history. For example, the Western is well represented by the protagonist, who embodies the archetypal 'man with no name' – an American cowboy/aimless drifter

Figure 6.1 *Dust Devil*

complete with hat, spurs and vernacular. However, the film also draws upon the horror genre with the use of extreme body horror and violence which in places seems to border on spoof-comedy.

The film was unlike anything that had been commissioned by the channel in the past, and it was for this reason that David Aukin made the decision to co-finance the production. Although *Dust Devil* took only £30,000 during its UK cinema run, the film represented, for Aukin at least, something more important. This was a call to the industry that the channel was now willing to accept a very different kind of script, and that Film on Four could commission genre films that could be populist, entertaining and targeted at a very different kind of audience. According to Aukin, whether accurate or not there was a perception in the industry that there was a 'type' of film that Channel 4 was more likely to accept; specifically, productions that fit into the 'worthy' social-realist mode. In a recent interview he stated that the commission caused filmmakers to take notice:

> I think suddenly the industry said, 'Fuck, he's doing *Dust Devil*'. You know, that's interesting, that's not something that we would expect Channel 4 to be doing. And it wasn't a particularly successful film … but nevertheless as a genre [piece] it gave a message out to the industry that I was interested in more than just social realism.[26]

The muddled styles of the film perhaps reflect the confusion and uncertainty of the time, namely, the question of whether the channel should fund more commercial, populist productions in light of recent industry changes, or whether it should even continue to offer films a theatrical release at all. At this early stage in his role as Head of Drama, Aukin was an unknown quantity to filmmakers. So, to some extent, was Film on Four, in terms of how well it would perform in the changing commercial market. The old debates about whether Film on Four made cinema films or simply jumped-up single plays were also still prevalent in the industry, and *Dust Devil* acted as a signpost for a change in the policy and direction of the channel's film financing activities.

However, it was Channel 4's commitment to the contemporary and the socially relevant which led Stephen Woolley to think that the channel would invest in *The Crying Game* without hesitation. *The Crying Game* was originally to be named *The Soldier's Wife*, and was conceived by Jordan and Woolley during their first meeting in 1982. However, productions such as *The Company of Wolves* and *The Miracle* (Neil Jordan, 1991) took precedence, and though Woolley kept promising to find finance for the film, the script remained in development until 1991.[27] The film follows Fergus (Stephen Rea), who is part of an IRA group that captures a black British soldier named Jody. Jody, who is about to be executed, asks Fergus

Figure 6.2 Fergus (Stephen Rea) and Dil (Jaye Davidson) in *The Crying Game*.

to seek out his girlfriend Dil after his death. Fergus falls in love with Dil, who is later revealed to be a transwoman, a fact which initially disgusts Fergus until he realises he still has feelings for her. When Dil shoots an IRA operative who has tracked Fergus down, Fergus frames himself for the murder and takes the fall. *The Crying Game*, widely viewed at the time of its release as progressive in its treatment of Fergus/Dil's relationship, has since come to occupy an ambiguous position within the canon of queer and LGBTQIA British cinema history. This is in part to do with the film's treatment of Fergus's reaction to Dil's sex, and in part to do with the marketing campaign Miramax ran to promote the film, which hinged entirely around audiences keeping the 'spoiler' of Dil's identity a secret because of the supposed shock factor among audiences the company hoped would result from this 'reveal'.

The production history of *The Crying Game* provides a detailed insight into the creative and editorial decision-making processes of the channel from script stage to post-production, as well as presenting a useful study of the channel's financial and cultural priorities regarding its own film-funding practices. David Aukin and Jack Lechner were initially impressed with the screenplay, stating that it was one of the best they had ever read, though they were less convinced by the ending, which they felt was an anti-climax.[28] They expressed concern that the IRA story drowned the love story, and that Dil's revelation would ultimately turn the film into a 'freak show'.[29] Their reservations were such that, according to Woolley, the film was turned down by the channel seventeen times. Woolley later admitted that 'It finally got to where I even threatened to immolate myself in the channel Four foyer'.[30] Certainly, if it were not for his persistence and unwavering belief in the script, the film might never have been made. Woolley had submitted *The Soldier's Wife* to many studios, but it was seen as too controversial. French company Ciby 2000 turned it down because of the sexual element, while Miramax loved it but wanted a woman to be cast in the role of Dil, which Woolley thought would be dishonest.[31] For Woolley, Channel 4 was the likeliest sponsor. He and Jordan submitted redraft after redraft, and though these were received enthusiastically, Aukin felt that the script was just not good enough.[32] In a last desperate bid to achieve funding, Woolley wrote a series of impassioned letters to the channel, trying to appeal to their sense of cultural provenance:

> If there is one shred of doubt that it *may* be a film you will later be proud of then do not pass up this opportunity … This letter is heartfelt and serious and if Palace has attained a clownish veneer it

masks its serious and passionate desire to see good work initiated, fulfilled and applauded if appropriate. This desire traverses the world of cinema from *When Harry Met Sally* to *Hairspray*, from *Rhapsody in August* to *Evil Dead* and from *Lenny Henry Live* to *Sid and Nancy*.[33]

Channel 4 finally agreed to fund the film, though the production was beset with financial troubles from the start. This was because Powell and Woolley took the same approach to financing with *The Crying Game* as they had with many other productions, which was to rush into shooting prematurely before all of the financing was completely in place and the production money had been released.

Without support from a Hollywood backer, the budget of *The Crying Game* was £2.3 million, down from £3 million after deferring the producers' fees.[34] Powell had trouble closing the production deals and unlocking finance, as Palace's completion guarantor would not sign off on location shooting in Ireland, which meant the production monies would not be released. This was exacerbated by the fact that Powell was also struggling to release the money for two other Palace productions that were shooting simultaneously, *Dust Devil* and *Waterland* (Stephen Gyllenhaal, 1992).[35] According to Woolley, the company 'begged, stole, and borrowed and I pushed my own credit card to the limit. Without the patience and support of British Screen and Channel 4, the movie would have closed down in a week or two.'[36] Palace's approach to raising finance was notoriously haphazard, and this was something that began to raise tensions within the channel. When Woolley wrote to Colin Leventhal asking for money to keep the production going, Leventhal replied:

> You write such good letters but you know, as well as I do, that *The Soldier's Wife* is the third in a line of films which started with *Dust Devil* and continued with *Waterland* in which the financing arrangements came together in a way which really would not be tolerated in any other business. I will have another look at our contracts on films purchased from Palace, and see what we might do, but frankly it is not going to begin to approach the sort of money you say you need to survive. It seems to me that your company has needed re-financing for some time and I can only hope that the necessary arrangements are completed within days.[37]

Financing was finally unlocked, though as the film was nearing completion Aukin and Lechner were still unsure about the ending. Powell later admitted to shooting an alternative 'happy' ending where the leads escaped to Barbados, simply in order to show the channel that it wouldn't work.[38] The channel did indeed agree that the re-shot ending was terrible, and gave the producers permission to re-shoot it according to the original script, at the cost of an additional £45,000.[39]

The distribution of *The Crying Game* will be explored in greater detail in Chapter 9. However, it is worth noting here that, through a combination of targeted marketing and word of mouth, *The Crying Game* went on to gross around $65 million in America, winning widespread critical acclaim and six Academy Award nominations, including Best Film and Best Director. The success of the film came too late for Palace, however; by March 1992, the company was going bust, through what Alexander Walker argues was a combination of 'bad luck, lack of capital, poor management that never really escaped from the "haphazard hippie idealism" that had been its foundation, an absence of ready-to-hand box-office hits and personal hubris'.[40] Palace was also suffering from a spate of over-production in the late 1980s from which it had never fully recovered. The company finally went into liquidation in August 1992, and its collapse deeply affected its many creditors. Despite Palace being unable to cash in on the film's success, *The Crying Game* was, for Woolley at least, lasting proof of the company's service to the industry:

> If any film were to encapsulate Palace's commitment to film production and British cinema then it would be *The Crying Game*. It was made against extreme prejudice, without any initial backing from the US and an apparent blindness to the combined track record of both Jordan and myself for producing relatively commercial films for below $5m … and in the Palace tradition, it tackles race, sexuality and politics within the framework of an accessible mainstream thriller.[41]

The success of the film did also go some way towards ensuring that Powell and Woolley's next company, Scala Productions, got off the ground.[42] With the help of Michael Kuhn, who appreciated the talents of the producers despite the collapse of their company, PFE negotiated a 'first look' deal with Scala in exchange for covering its overheads.[43] Through Scala, Powell and Woolley went on to collaborate with Channel 4 on *Backbeat* (Iain Softley, 1994), *The Neon Bible* (Terence Davies, 1995) and *Hollow Reed* (Angela Pope, 1996). The producers also felt a certain amount of loyalty towards the channel, as evidenced by a clash between BSkyB and the channel's interest during the financing of *Hollow Reed*. Both companies wanted to purchase the television rights to the film, but as Powell stated, 'our [Woolley and Powell's] relationship is firmly with Channel 4 (with whom we have produced over ten films), and there's no way we would jump ship to BskyB for whom we have never produced a film'.[44]

The production of *The Crying Game* provides an illuminating example of the creative and practical issues faced by Channel 4 Commissioning Editors as well as exploring the channel's working relationships with film producers. The film's production history offers an insight into the cultural motivations of a company like Palace, particularly in terms of the persistence of producer Stephen Woolley in obtaining funding. Given the nature of the industry, long-term success stories of British film production companies are few and far between. However, the next section will focus on the channel's relationship with a company with which it enjoyed a productive relationship creatively and financially, as a means of exploring the long-term financial and editorial support the channel could offer to British producers.

Working Title Films

Initially headed by Sarah Radclyffe and Tim Bevan, Working Title achieved its first big success with its debut feature-length production, *My Beautiful Laundrette*, which was fully funded by Channel 4, and the company continued to seek out production partnerships with the channel throughout the 1980s. Both Film on Four and Working Title underwent corporate reorganisation in the early 1990s, as Channel 4 prepared to adapt to a more commercial broadcasting environment and Working Title was bought by the film arm of the multinational conglomerate PolyGram. One consequence of these changes was fewer production partnerships, though *Four Weddings and a Funeral* and *Elizabeth* (Shekhar Kapur, 1992), both part-funded by Channel 4, were notable commercial successes. Tim Bevan cites Channel 4 as one of Working Title's more consistent supporters,[45] and the following case study will examine the importance of the channel to the development of Working Title in terms of its impact on the British film industry both economically and culturally, while also exploring the ways in which both Channel 4 films and Working Title evolved in response to a changing industry. In 1998 Working Title solidified its relationship with Hollywood following a take-over by Universal, while Film on Four became FilmFour and began to invest in more ambitious projects under Paul Webster.

Producers Tim Bevan and Sarah Radclyffe came together in 1984 to form pop promo company Aldabra with the eventual aim of raising enough finance to fund the production of feature films. Pop videos were profitable enterprises for established directors at a time when the industry was in decline, and for Bevan and Radclyffe, making music videos also led to relationships with directors such as Derek Jarman, Nicolas Roeg and most importantly Stephen Frears, who first approached Bevan with the script for *My Beautiful Laundrette*.[46] Following the success of *Laundrette*, Working Title eked out a meagre living producing films on extremely tight budgets. Many of these productions were made in partnership with Channel 4, such as Stephen Frears's *Sammy and Rosie Get Laid* (1987), *Wish You Were Here* (David Leland, 1987), *A World Apart* (Chris Menges, 1988), *Diamond Skulls* (Nick Broomfield, 1989), *Fools of Fortune* (Pat O'Connor, 1990), *Smack and Thistle* (Tunde Ikoli, 1991) and *Dakota Road* (Nick Ward, 1991). None of these films were commercial hits, but due to the strict budgeting of Bevan and Radclyffe they did at least break even or make some profit.

Relationship with PolyGram

In the early 1990s, music company PolyGram was looking to diversify into film under the direction of Michael Kuhn. Following a chance meeting between Kuhn and Bevan, PolyGram invested 49% in Working Title in 1989 and eventually bought the company as one of its indie 'labels' in 1992, along with Propaganda Films and Jodie Foster's company Egg Pictures.[47] This restructuring precipitated a change for Working Title in terms of its business practices and the nature of the company's output. The changing landscape of British production in the 1980s and the harsh realities of working on low-budget features led to Bevan and Radclyffe realising divergent ambitions. Bevan believed that in order to build a successful company, films must have commercial appeal, but for Radclyffe, this change would necessitate compromise, and the creative freedom of working within low budgets was preferable. As Bevan stated in an interview in 1993,

> this restructuring means that we have made a change in our focus, we have been known more for art house films in the past. Now, with the full-backing of PolyGram, we will be pushing for bigger-budget, more commercial fare. Sarah likes the more intimate film.[48]

When PolyGram took over Working Title, Radclyffe left to form her own company and Eric Fellner, previously of Initial Films, stepped in to replace her as co-partner.[49]

PolyGram Filmed Entertainment (PFE), as the new film arm of PolyGram was named, owned film production companies in much the same way that its parent company owned music 'labels'. This was a system that Kuhn had copied from the music industry and which in theory allowed for a great deal of creative autonomy on the part of the 'labels' in question.[50] Working Title was initially seen as a 'crappy arthouse label' with the real winners seen to be Egg Pictures, although the company soon achieved breakthrough success with *Four Weddings*.[51] Throughout the 1990s Working Title retained around thirty to forty staff and had three main arms: development, business and physical production, with bases both in London and Los Angeles. Film production would normally take three forms. The first was third-party involvement, in which Working Title would oversee the production and distribution, provide some finance and offer some creative opinion. This very much characterised Working Title's involvement in the films of the Coen brothers. The second type was productions in which Working Title had complete creative involvement from script to screen – i.e. books or screenplays bought and then turned into scripts. The third type would be original ideas or scripts developed by the company. Productions of this kind included Lawrence Kasdan's *French Kiss* (1995) and Shekhar Kapur's *Elizabeth*.[52] Existing within PFE allowed Working Title to take bigger financial risks, while the company also had the advantage of the much sought-after access to American distribution through PFE's US distribution arm, Gramercy Pictures. However, as Bevan points out, despite operating within the studio system the company has always maintained creative autonomy: 'I think there is, in a funny way, a "Working Title movie" and that's got nothing to do with what Michael Kuhn at Polygram or Stacey Snider at Universal or anyone else has said to us along the way.'[53] Both Bevan and Fellner see themselves as 'creative producers' seeking collaborative relationships between writer, director and producer and professing that the attribution of authorship to a film under the director has been 'much abused' and 'bad for business'.[54] Working within the studio system has allowed Working Title to become the only company to successfully negotiate production arms in both the UK and the USA. With numerous international successes including *Four Weddings, Bean* (Mel Smith, 1997), *Notting Hill* (Roger Michell,

1999) and *Bridget Jones's Diary* (Sharon Maguire, 2001), the company generated £1.12 billion between 1992 and 2004.[55]

My Beautiful Laundrette

My Beautiful Laundrette is generally acknowledged as the film that gave birth to Working Title. Discussing his time on the production, Stephen Frears extends this 'birthing' metaphor:

> I feel like a taxi driver who's had a baby born in the back of his cab and had to work as a midwife. Making *My Beautiful Laundrette* was joyful, messy, alive; there was no epidural, no blood-letting, no episiotomy. I had no idea the baby would grow up to be the most successful company in the history of British cinema. What larks![56]

Karin Bamborough had originally approached Hanif Kureishi to write the script, which was funded through the Film on Four Script Development Fund. Kureishi then posted the script to Stephen Frears, who asked Tim Bevan to produce it while he was working on a music video for Aldabra. Initially, the wait for production would have been around a year, although luckily another film was dropped from Channel 4's slate at this time and *Laundrette* was the ideal choice to replace it.[57] The film was a resounding success, crossing over from television to cinema and securing a distribution deal in the USA. The plot centres on Omar, a Pakistani, and Johnny, his working-class school friend and an ex-neo-Nazi. The two men become lovers and decide to renovate Omar's uncle's run-down laundrette using drug money. The film opened to critical success and enjoyed an extended run in many cinemas in the UK, while *Screen International* called the film a 'runaway arthouse hit' in America, where it grossed $751, 465.[58] The film premiered on Channel 4 in 1987, gaining ratings of 4.3 million on its first run and 3.5 million on its second.[59] Jeremy Isaacs argues that it was the timing of *My Beautiful Laundrette* and the talents which came together on the production that contributed to its success:

> *My Beautiful Laundrette* captured a moment in Britain, which is one of those things filmmaking is for. And it gave audiences in the cinema and on television great pleasure, which is the other. To see it on our screen and to know that we had put it there and that millions were now enjoying it was rather satisfying.[60]

Figure 6.3   *My Beautiful Laundrette*

Culturally, the film is often cited as pushing forward the boundaries of black and Asian filmmaking in its defiance to portray racial stereotypes, serving as an inspiration for directors like Isaac Julien (*Young Soul Rebels*, 1991) and Gurinder Chadha (*Bhaji on the Beach*, 1993) and writers like Ayub Khan Din (*East is East*, Damien O'Donnell, 1999).[61]

My Beautiful Laundrette is often described as being the 'archetypal Film on Four', but it could just as easily be described as the 'archetypal Working Title film' of this era. Indeed, many of Working Title's subsequent projects were characterised as 'socio-economic and political movies with a strong narrative'.[62] A continuing relationship with Channel 4 and writer Kureishi formed the basis of two further collaborations. *Sammy and Rosie Get Laid* was also funded by Channel 4 and relatively well received, although it did not garner positive critical responses on the same level as *Laundrette*. However, it shared many similar themes and characters: Rafi, a beguiling, warm-hearted but morally suspect patriarch (Sammy's father), two central characters in a love relationship, a political background that drew heavily upon aspects of contemporary ethnic life in London, and a cynical analysis of middle class-liberalism. However, the formula was too carnivalesque for many reviewers, and Leonard Quart characterised it as being a 'work of excess, both in its form and content . . . a bouncy, vibrant film too crammed with themes, characters and cuts'.[63] Hanif Kureishi made his directorial debut in *London Kills Me* (1991) which tells the story of Clint, a member of a drug-dealing posse who decides to go straight and is offered a job by a restaurant manager on the condition that he finds a decent pair of shoes. The film again focuses on similar issues, although it was critically panned for betraying a distinct lack of tension and poor character development.

Working with Channel 4

Between 1989 and 1992, PolyGram owned 49% of Working Title, and many of the Channel 4-funded films produced in this period were designed to test the relationship between Working Title and PFE.[64] Films such as *Diamond Skulls, Fools of Fortune, Smack and Thistle* and *Dakota Road* were low-budget features compared to later Working Title productions, and Kuhn dismisses these films as 'a slew of bad and unsuccessful movies' made at a time when Working Title was trying to get a decent development slate on track in anticipation of the move to PolyGram.[65] However, these early Channel 4 partnerships had gained Working Title a reputation for reliability, a factor that Tim Bevan credits with influencing bigger companies to place within him a certain amount of trust. By 1994, Working Title had produced twenty films (nine of which were funded by Channel 4), marking Bevan and Fellner out as experienced producers. Many of the early Channel 4/Working Title partnerships were thus important to the future development of the company, as was the success of a hit like *My Beautiful Laundrette*. According to Tim Bevan:

> [Film on Four] got us started basically. And those early movies, you know, the half a dozen, six, seven, eight pictures that they invested in, that we were able to cut our teeth on, within a comfortable environment … really it's a sort of textbook and perfect example of what should happen from subsidised backing, you know where you learn your trade and then you go out and find somebody who can commercially back you.[66]

Tim Bevan stated that Working Title owed its existence to Channel 4 for this reason, as before the company was taken under the wing of PolyGram, 'interest in British work [was] … impossible to find. To have received that sort of support throughout the Eighties has amounted to a kind of miracle.'[67]

Working Title also provided Channel 4 with a strong slate of films, as David Rose attests:

> While I was head of drama in Channel 4's early days and running Film on Four in the eighties, people were always asking what it was we were looking for in the films we commissioned. It was a tough question … I didn't feel it was our job to be prescriptive about Film on Four. Once Working Title had produced a number of features for the channel, their distinctive body of work provided one answer to that question.[68]

Under PFE, Working Title was able to overcome many of the problems endemic to independent British film companies. The company now had access to the US distributor Gramercy as well as the financial backing which allowed it to spend more time on pre-production. The early 1990s can be seen as a turning point for the company, and with the move to PolyGram and the departure of Sarah Radclyffe, its focus shifted towards more commercially viable filmmaking. At the same time, Channel 4 was beginning the transition, under Michael Grade, to selling its own advertising, and the focus of the channel slowly shifted towards more mainstream, popular programming. Though Film on Four was able to continue under David Aukin, attitudes towards film financing among television executives at the channel became more favourable following a string of commercial successes in the mid-1990s beginning with *Shallow Grave* (Danny Boyle, 1994), then *Four Weddings and a Funeral*, *Trainspotting* (Boyle, 1996), *East is East* and many others.[69] David Wood also argues that the breakdown in the relationship between Channel 4 and British Screen in the mid-1990s led to:

> A new set of partnerships … that have enabled the channel to get involved in glossier, bigger budget productions. Films funded by wealthy US distributors or UK based entertainment groups such as PolyGram Filmed Entertainment enable Channel 4 to bask in the reflected glory of hit films without taking the financial risks.[70]

The British film industry has historically dealt with the challenge of Hollywood in two ways: by producing low-budget features aimed at a British market, or by striving to produce larger-budget features with high production values in order to make a profit in the US market. In the 1990s, there was a general impetus towards the latter. Paul Dave also argues that Working Title's post-1980s history displayed 'the contemporary alignment of the British Film industry with, in the words of co-chairman Eric Fellner, "filmmaking as a global business".[71]

Four Weddings and a Funeral

Four Weddings and a Funeral was Working Title's first truly 'global' film. Originally intended to be a Channel 4 production, pre-production had been abandoned for 'creative reasons'.[72] The original budget was £2.9 million, of which Channel 4 contributed around £1 million. Working Title had developed a good relationship with Richard Curtis on *The Tall Guy* (Mel Smith, 1989), so much so that Curtis decided to approach the company with the script for *Four Weddings*.[73] Maggie Brown suggests that PFE did not want to fund the title fully because Hugh Grant was an unknown quantity overseas, and so it allowed Channel 4 to provide a significant amount of the budget.[74] PFE marketing executive Peter Graves devised a strategy that was unusual at the time but has been much copied since. The company planned to open the film in the USA rather than the UK, the reasoning being that if the film opened in the UK and flopped, there was only a very small chance that it would achieve success internationally.[75] To minimise advertising costs, the film was given a 'platform' release, a distribution method common to small independent US companies whereby a film would be released on just a few screens and then slowly expanded to more cinemas based on the success of word-of-mouth marketing. *Four Weddings* was initially released solely in New York and Los Angeles and opened on just five screens, performing successfully enough for this to be gradually broadened over a period of weeks to approximately 700 screens around the country.[76] Internationally the film eventually made around $200 million, although Nigel Mather suggests that the relationship between Channel 4 and Working Title may have been soured by these financial returns. Michael Grade had initially claimed that the channel would receive around £4 million for its investment. However, during a government Select Committee meeting to discuss the state of the film industry in 1995, Labour MP Joe Ashton suggested that Channel 4 had been 'taken to the cleaners' considering the massive financial success of the film. Michael Kuhn responded to these claims with vitriol: 'Channel 4 puts 2p into our films and then complains when they get £5 million back, so screw them.'[77] Nevertheless, Channel 4 was able to reap the success of the film when the television premiere gained twelve million viewers, still the highest rating in the channel's history.[78]

The winning formula of *Four Weddings* and the Working Title/Richard Curtis relationship led to a series of now characteristic 'Working Title films'. *Notting Hill* (which was begun under PFE in 1998 and moved to Universal along with Working Title), *Bridget Jones's Diary* and *Love Actually* (Richard Curtis, 2003) form a series of romantic comedies that have been much criticised for portraying an idealised white middle-class view of Britain to an international audience. This is a world where idiosyncratic, floppy-haired aristocrats inhabit English town houses in areas of London where ethnic minorities have mysteriously ceased to exist.[79] Shortly after the release of *Notting Hill* Tim Dowling wrote an article entitled 'Curtis' Britain' in which he comments:

> The largest proportion [of characters] will naturally have gone to either Oxford or Cambridge, in keeping with the fact that approximately 70% of the population attended one or the other … English people rarely go into work, and if they do they generally carry out their jobs with an endearing incompetence. They just happen to believe there are more important things in life, like swearing and snow.[80]

Nick James argues that when British films are aimed at a global marketplace they defer to American notions of 'Britishness' and the series of films produced following the success of *Four Weddings* bolstered this idea with their celebration of traditional notions of British reserve and self-deprecation.[81] Tim Bevan has long propounded the idea that in order to produce successful British films a company needs a marketable product and a good relationship with Hollywood. However, he has also argued that this relationship does not have to be at the expense of engagement with British politics and culture. Before the release of *My Beautiful Laundrette*, Bevan stated in an article for *AIP&Co* that in order to achieve a healthy industry

> producers should be guiding the creativity in the film world into making films that are of a broad interest and entertaining … [and] if *My Beautiful Laundrette*, a film about a gay Pakistani Laundrette owner, can find US distribution then the area for commercial success is very wide.[82]

However, *Laundrette* only received a very limited theatrical release, and subsequent Working Title films marketed in the USA have shown that the company's relationship with Hollywood 'necessitates a compromise, smoothing away the specifically British aspects of the subject'.[83] Annabel Roe argues that the British film industry has long been uncomfortable with Working Title's relationship with the USA for this reason, with many critics regarding them as 'commercial sell-outs to Hollywood'.[84] Perhaps this is evidence of underlying tensions within the company regarding the limits of creative freedom. Working Title has always had the power to 'greenlight' projects from within the studio system, but it was a necessary pre-requisite for Michael Khun that these films should be commercially viable overseas. Under PFE the company thus relinquished the freedom to make the riskier social-political dramas that had been the hallmark of its partnerships with Channel 4 in the 1980s.

The international success of films like *Four Weddings* brought increased confidence to the British film industry, and the next Working Title/Channel 4 collaboration, *Elizabeth*, was produced at the height of that confidence. Though the channel did not have any editorial input on *Elizabeth*, it had previously co-produced *The Madness of King George* (Nicholas Hytner, 1994), and the success of this film directly influenced Working Title's decision to produce *Elizabeth*. PFE executive Julia Short said, 'we did a great deal of research into previous costume dramas, and we took *The Madness of King George* as our ruler'.[85] *Elizabeth* was one of a number of historical biopics produced in the 1990s similar to *King George*, and the BBC had funded John Madden's *Mrs Brown* (1997), although this took a radically different approach to the genre.[86] *Elizabeth* is a conspiratorial thriller that is more in keeping with *The Godfather* (Francis Ford Coppola, 1972) in visual style than with Merchant Ivory productions. Indeed, Tim Bevan stated that the Working Title team watched *The Godfather* for ideas as to how to structure the film.[87] The development of *Elizabeth* was thus consciously radical on the part of the producers, and this was further exemplified by their choice of director. Shekhar Kapur had never made an English-language film, and his previous film, *Bandit Queen* (1994), was so violent and sexually explicit that it was banned by the Indian censors.

Bandit Queen had been funded by Channel 4, and this had perhaps influenced the choice of Kapur as director.[88] Kapur's style is undoubtedly reflected in the style of the film, with its fast-paced editing less reticent than that of Merchant Ivory productions, obtrusively tracking characters around onscreen rather than distancing itself from them.[89] *Elizabeth* falls into the category of films that Church Gibson notes as 'post-heritage', along with productions such as *Shakespeare in Love* (John Madden, 1998) and *The Wings of the Dove* (Iain Softley, 1997).[90] *Sight and Sound* characterised the film as 'a far cry from the sterility of British heritage movies … But what Kapur does do is capture the age's intensity and oddity … its otherness from us as well as him'.[91] James Chapman draws parallels between *Elizabeth* and Alexander Korda's *The Private Life of Henry VIII* (1933) by noting that the film is populist rather than stuffy and seeks to re-mould the historical biopic for younger audiences.[92]

Partnerships between Channel 4 and Working Title were less frequent by the late 1990s. However, although *Four Weddings* and *Elizabeth* can be seen as being among the most culturally significant productions to come out of the Channel 4/Working Title relationship, the influence of the channel can be most strongly identified throughout the first seven years of Working Title's life, and it was partly through the support and encouragement of Channel 4 that this small independent eventually became one of the most successful production companies in British history.

Conclusion

Living from film to film and trying to raise finance from disparate sources with no guarantee of distribution was the norm for independent producers working in Britain at this time, without the backing of a major studio, and with little in the way of tax breaks or government sponsorship in place. Palace was unusual in having access to its own distribution arm, and this contributed to its many successes, even though the company eventually collapsed due to a combination of over-production and mismanagement. However, though sustainability was difficult to find, for companies like Working Title, Channel 4 did provide a relatively consistent source of funding, working with the company throughout a decade when the industry was in constant decline. Additionally, as well as maintaining a commitment to training new writing and directorial talent, the channel also acted as a training ground for many new independent companies, operating efficient and detailed systems of cost control and also offering the benefit of years of experience in dealing with other independents, co-financiers and distributors.

Notes

1. Angus Finney, *The Egos Have Landed: The Rise and Fall of Palace Pictures* (London: William Heinemann, 1996), 43.
2. Phil Wickham, *Back to the Future: The Fall and Rise of the British Film Industry in the 1980s* (London: BFI, 2005), 15.
3. Finney, *The Egos Have Landed*.

4. Anon., 'Palace Through the Looking Glass?', *Screen International*, 7 May 1992, 12.
5. Wickham, *Back to the Future*, 15.
6. Finney, *The Egos Have Landed*, 79.
7. *Ibid.*, 123.
8. *The Independent*, 8 November 1992.
9. Stephen Woolley, personal communication, 22 March 2012.
10. Helen de Winter, *'What I Really Want to Do Is Produce …': Top Producers Talk Movies and Money* (London: Faber & Faber, 2006), 70.
11. Finney, *The Egos Have Landed*, 83.
12. *The Independent*, 19 December 1997.
13. Finney, *The Egos Have Landed*, 67–8.
14. Stephen Woolley, personal communication, 22 March 2012.
15. *Ibid.*
16. Chris Salewicz, 'Moscow on the Mersey', *Time Out* (Oct/Dec 1985).
17. *Ibid.*
18. Finney, *The Egos Have Landed*, 124–5.
19. Stephen Woolley, personal communication, 22 March 2012.
20. *Ibid.*
21. Hilary Brown, 'The Film Man', *Airwaves*, 13 (Winter 1987/88), 23.
22. Graham Wade, 'Powell's Picture Palace', *Stills* (March 1985), 38–41.
23. *The Observer*, 4 February 1990.
24. James Saynor, 'Writers' Television', *Sight and Sound*, 2:7 (November 1992), 30.
25. Paul Bonner with Leslie Aston, *Independent Television in Britain Volume 6: New Developments in Independent Television, 1981–92: Channel 4, TV-am, Cable and Satellite* (Basingstoke: Palgrave, 2003), 198.
26. David Aukin, personal communication, 23 February 2012.
27. Finney, *The Egos Have Landed*, 6.
28. *Ibid.*, 21.
29. *Ibid.*
30. *Christian Science Monitor*, 26 March 1993.
31. Alexander Walker, *Icons in the Fire: The Rise and Fall of Practically Everyone in the British Film Industry 1984–2000* (London: Orion, 2004), 149.
32. Finney, *The Egos Have Landed*, 20–1.
33. *Ibid.*
34. Walker, *Icons in the Fire*, 149.
35. Finney, *The Egos Have Landed*, 23.
36. *Time Out*, 4 November 1992.
37. Finney, *The Egos Have Landed*, 26.
38. *Ibid.*
39. *Ibid.*
40. Walker, *Icons in the Fire*, 151.
41. *Time Out*, 4 November 1992.
42. *The Guardian*, 1 November 1996.
43. Walker, *Icons in the Fire*, 152.
44. Nik Powell, 'The Producer', in *Inside Stories: Diaries of British Filmmakers at Work*, ed. by Duncan Petrie (London: BFI Publishing, 1996).

45. Working Title, *Laundrettes and Lovers: From Storyboard to Billboard* (London: Boxtree Ltd, 2003), 11.

46. *AIP & Co*, 71, January/February (1986), 22–4.

47. Michael Kuhn, *One Hundred Films and a Funeral: The Life and Death of PolyGram Films* (London: Thorogood, 2003), 33–5.

48. *Daily Variety*, 8 February 1993.

49. *The Guardian*, 15 December 1993.

50. Kuhn, *One Hundred Films*, 33.

51. *Variety*, 14 December 1998.

52. Working Title, *Laundrettes and Lovers*, 18.

53. de Winter, '*What I Really Want to Do Is Produce*', 99.

54. *Ibid.*

55. BBC News Website. Available at <http://news.bbc.co.uk/1/hi/entertainment/2821801.stm> (accessed 16 February 2004).

56. Working Title, *Laundrettes and Lovers*, 35.

57. *Ibid.*

58. Christine Geraghty, *My Beautiful Laundrette* (New York: I. B. Tauris, 2004), 16.

59. *Ibid.*, 16.

60. Bonner with Aston, *Independent Television*, 199.

61. *Ibid.*, 77–9.

62. Paul Dave, *Visions of England: Class and Culture in Contemporary Cinema* (Oxford: Bloomsbury, 2006), 40.

63. Leonard Quart, 'Sammy and Rosie Get Laid,' *Cineaste*, 16:4 (1987), 47.

64. Kuhn, *One Hundred Films*, 38.

65. *Ibid.*, 38.

66. de Winter, *Top Producers*, 99.

67. *The Observer*, 4 February 1990.

68. Working Title, *Laundrettes and Lovers*, 29.

69. Maggie Brown, *A Licence to Be Different: The Story of Channel 4* (London: BFI Publishing, 2007), 189–91.

70. Anne Jäckel, 'Broadcasters' Involvement in Co-Productions', in *Television Broadcasting in Contemporary France and Britain*, ed. by Michael Scriven (New York: Berghahn Books, 1999), 175–97, 180.

71. Dave, *Visions of England*, 54.

72. Kuhn, *One Hundred Films*, 58.

73. Working Title, *Laundrettes and Lovers*, 14.

74. Brown, *A Licence to Be Different*, 190.

75. Kuhn, *One Hundred Films*, 61.

76. *Ibid.*, 62.

77. Quoted in Nigel Mather, *Tears of Laughter: Comedy Drama in 1990s British Cinema* (Manchester: Manchester University Press, 2006), 150–1.

78. Accessed from http://www.Channel4.com/media/documents/corporate/foi-docs/4_at_20.pdf

79. Annabel Honess Roe, 'A "Special Relationship?" The Coupling of Britain and America in Working Title's Romantic Comedies', in *Falling in Love Again: Romantic Comedy in Contemporary Cinema*, ed. by Stacey Abbott (London: I. B. Tauris, 2009), 77–88, 81.

80. *The Guardian*, 13 November 2003. Available at: <http://www.guardian.co.uk/film/2003/nov/13/britishidentity.uk> (accessed 20 September 2023).

81. Nick James, 'They Think It's All Over: British Cinema's US Surrender', in *The British Cinema, Book* ed. by Robert Murphy, 2nd edn (London: BFI Publishing, 2001), 303.

82. *AIP&Co*, 71, January/February (1986), 23.

83. James, 'They Think It's All Over', 306.

84. Roe, 'A "Special Relationship?"', 81.

85. James Chapman, Past and Present: National Identity and the British Historical Film (London: I. B. Tauris, 2005), 302.

86. *Ibid.*, 299.

87. Working Title, *Laundrettes and Lovers*, 51.

88. Chapman, Past and Present, 302.

89. *Ibid.*, 305.

90. Dave, *Visions of England*, 40.

91. *Sight and Sound*, 8:11 (November 1998), 47.

92. Chapman, Past and Present, 305.

Chapter 7

Short films and shallow graves

This chapter will look at Film on Four's relationship with filmmakers and its initiatives to work with, encourage and find new talent, while examining the place of the Drama Department within the wider organisational structure of the channel. The tension between creativity and commercial constraint in broadcasting has been the subject of many academic studies, but how profound was this tension, specifically within Channel 4? Perhaps the answer to this question is far more ambiguous than has previously been assumed – rather than creative 'constraint' in this context, a better phrase might be creative 'negotiation'. Furthermore, what are the conditions in which talent is sought out and developed? In order to explore these questions, this chapter will offer a case study of Danny Boyle's 1994 film *Shallow Grave* which will provide an analysis of the ways in which David Aukin and his team worked with individual filmmakers. This case study will also seek to explore the relationship between Film on Four and upper management at the channel, arguing that the success of individual productions could determine policy and decision-making on an executive level. Supporting new filmmakers was a part of Film on Four's remit from its beginnings in 1982, and with this in mind, this chapter will examine the effectiveness of Channel 4's short-film strand, Short and Curlies (1987–1995), in finding and supporting new filmmaking talent. This short study will also offer an insight into an oft-neglected aspect of film scholarship: namely, the importance of contacts, informal networks and relationships in film production.

Shallow Grave and the new creative culture of the 1990s

The number of projects which came to fruition through personal contact and informal conversations (as opposed to unsolicited scripts) hints at the ambiguous nature of Film on Four's position between broadcasting and the film industry. The Drama Department was operating as a commissioner of television programming through Film on Four, but it was also engaging with a large informal network of film industry contacts. Allon Reich, Assistant Commissioning Editor for Film between 1994 and 1998, states that because he was working predominantly with film producers, writers and directors, 'I felt much more like I was working in the film industry . . . So I knew the people – colleagues – in Channel 4 but I only knew them because they worked in Channel 4 . . . I never felt that was my job.'[1] Aukin characterised television and film as being distinct communities, with those at the Drama Department having to negotiate both worlds:

> I think there was something very nourishing about being part of a wider community, and so you know the film world is quite a tight, you know, enclosed community anyway, and to have, to be able to think outside that box, to live in an environment that wasn't just obsessed with film I think is quite healthy and enabled you to take in all sorts of other influences and ideas.[2]

In commissioning a script for production, relationships and informal meetings and discussions were just as important as established process, if not more so. And, as the production history behind *Shallow Grave* illustrates, a commission could simply be the result of being in the right place at the right time.

In 1994 David Aukin commissioned *Shallow Grave*, made by the collaborative team of Andrew Macdonald, John Hodge and Danny Boyle, who then went on to work on *Trainspotting* with the channel in 1996 and *A Life Less Ordinary* in 1997. This film can give us an important insight into how Channel 4 encouraged and worked with new filmmaking talent. It was also extremely influential in shaping attitudes to Film on Four on the part of the channel's top executives, while its success at the domestic box office can also provide an insight into the increasing importance of Film on Four to the channel's own brand identity. As has already been noted, the broadcasting culture at Channel 4 changed gradually from the 1980s to the 1990s, which was due to a number of factors. When David Aukin left the channel in 1997, he published a series of letters in *The Guardian* that he had written to his son over the years, detailing his experiences at the channel. In one extract, he wrote:

> Today, October 1, 1990, I started at C4. Asked for all existing statistics about the films they'd commissioned since year zero and was somewhat surprised to find, when the information arrived, there is

> no mention of audience figures on TV transmission. When I asked for
> this, my new colleagues were clearly appalled at the request. Their
> beloved Film On 4 is now in the hands of a populist and vulgarian.
> Help![3]

This indicates that a polarisation between creative and commercial elements at the channel was more evident in its early days. As Roberts argues, from the early 1990s onwards, commercial thinking became more ingrained in day-to-day processes in broadcasting in general. For Channel 4, this shift towards increased commercialism can be characterised as a gradual process, over a period of several years – a period fraught with anxiety about the ability of the channel to drum up enough advertising revenue after 1993 to stay afloat.

Television executives at the channel were also uncertain about whether Film on Four could survive in the new, more commercial environment. In a way, *Shallow Grave* represented a real turning point for the strand. The film tells the story of three middle-class flatmates living in Edinburgh who decide to recruit a fourth housemate only to find him dead shortly afterwards, having left behind a big pile of cash. They decide to keep the money and bury the body in the shallow grave of the film's title. Though Michael Grade reacted badly to the film during an early private screening, dubbing it 'untransmittable', it became the first Film on Four in years to recoup its costs at the domestic box office. At the Dinard Film Festival in 1994 Michael Grade presented Macdonald, Hodge and Boyle with the

Figure 7.1 *Shallow Grave*

award for Best Film. According to Allon Reich, Grade 'turned up with two huge bottles of magnum champagne and said "well, that shows you what I know about film".[4] This was a defining moment for Film on Four in many ways, not least because, according to Reich, Michael Grade never looked at a cut of anything Film on Four produced again.[5] The success of the film strengthened the position of Film on Four within the channel, and, as we shall see, along with films like *Four Weddings and a Funeral* and *Trainspotting*, *Shallow Grave* became an important part of the identity and branding of Channel 4 in this period.

The process of commissioning a Film on Four had not, in theory, changed much since the channel's inception. Support for filmmakers was based on a pre-established commissioning system and a complex network of relationships. As the production history behind *Shallow Grave* illustrates, commissions could also simply be the result of luck. In 1993, David Aukin attended an industry conference in Inverness where producer Andrew Macdonald reportedly slipped Aukin's driver a five-pound note and the script for *Shallow Grave*, hoping that he would hand it over. According to Aukin, he read the script on the plane back to London simply because he didn't have anything else to read, and was so impressed that he decided to commission it. In 1993 Channel 4 agreed to finance the film to the amount of £850,000 on the condition that the Glasgow Film Fund would contribute the other £150,000.[6] All that remained was to find someone to direct it. Andrew Macdonald and John Hodge tried an unconventional approach to the situation, deciding to audition directors for the job. The script was sent to twenty directors, many of whom turned it down because the main characters were too unsympathetic, while some directors failed to make the cut because they wanted to make too many changes to the script. Danny Boyle won acceptance by describing the script as 'clean, mean and truly cinematic' and drawing comparisons to *Blood Simple* (Joel and Ethan Coen, 1984) in its commitment to narrative and plot. With the core team of producer, writer and director in place, the script was then redrafted and perfected with the help of Aukin and his team. Overall, Boyle described the relationship with the channel as supportive but not restrictive, stating that it 'worked well'.

> We all agreed that we'd like the plot to be more complex, which is something Channel 4 was pushing for as well. They were exemplary in the way they dealt with [us] – they kept hitting us with good strong suggestions, but we were free to use them or not.[7]

Hodge, Macdonald and Boyle planned at the outset to take equal creative credit for their films, travelling the festival circuit together and doing press interviews as a trio rather than individually. The team, particularly Macdonald, were concerned to replicate a long tradition of collaboration among British writers, producers and directors, often citing examples of longstanding partnerships like that between Powell and Pressburger and, more recently, Stephen Woolley and Neil Jordan as influences. Indeed, Hodge's energetic writing style and Macdonald's commercial sensibilities considerably influenced the style and direction of both films. In Boyle's case the desire to work more collaboratively may have been influenced by his background as a theatre director. Boyle's first job was with co-operative theatre company Joint Stock. He wanted to continue to work this way, so suggested that the team should share fees and profit equally.[8] The same team, from technical crew to cinematographer, were also asked to work together on *Trainspotting*. A collaboration of this nature was fairly unusual, but it was something that Aukin and his team sought to accommodate. This 'team effort' was something that Macdonald and Boyle promoted in the publicity for their films, underlining the effort of the designers and other personnel. While *Shallow Grave* and *Trainspotting* are commonly thought of as 'Danny Boyle films', an effort was made on the part of the principal team to reinforce the collaborative nature of production and challenge the established notion among critics that creativity in film is the province of a select few such as the writer and director.

In 1994 *Variety* noted the rise of a new generation of British film directors who had made their reputations in theatre.[9] Ex-Royal Court director Antonia Bird made waves with the BBC-funded film *Priest*, while Nick Hamm was making *Talk of Angels* for Miramax. Aukin, as a former executive director of the National Theatre, played a role in encouraging stage directors to cross over.[10] In addition to Danny Boyle on *Shallow Grave*, Nicholas Hytner made his feature debut, *The Madness of King George* (1994), through Film on Four, while Nancy Meckler directed the acclaimed Channel 4 film *Sister, My Sister* (1994). Actors had traditionally crossed back and forth between theatre and film, but this was less the norm for stage directors. This was perhaps because union restrictions in the 1980s prevented stage directors from crossing over easily, but a loosening of these rules in the 1990s resulted in a noticeable trend. Aukin, who had amassed considerable experience during his own time working in theatre, felt that stage directors could bring their own particular strengths to filmmaking; namely, an innate understanding of narrative and the ability to work well with actors.

One way in which Danny Boyle sought to facilitate a good relationship with Ewan McGregor, Kerry Fox and Christopher Eccleston on *Shallow Grave* was during the rehearsal stage. Boyle and the three actors moved into a flat during their one rehearsal week; they lived there, rehearsed, and invited people to pretend to 'audition' for the flat as part of a strategy to make them feel more comfortable playing flatmates. This is a strategy that Aukin continued to support, as Boyle used it again on *Trainspotting*, encouraging the actors and the crew to spend as much social time together as possible. According to Aukin, the skills of a former theatre director could be valuable because 'when we're working with theatre directors, I know we can assist them in virtually every technical area, give them great cameramen and designers, but the area where you cannot help a director is how to talk to an actor'.[11] After *Shallow Grave*, the team was inundated by lucrative deals from Hollywood (Boyle famously turned down an offer to direct *Alien: Resurrection* [Jean-Pierre Jeunet, 1997]) but decided to stick together to make an adaptation of Irvine Welsh's cult book *Trainspotting*. Channel 4 had provided the development funds for the film before *Shallow Grave* was released.

Working within low-budget filmmaking could be a constraining but positive force. Indeed, in interviews, Boyle often talked about the 'siege mentality' among a crew when working on a low-budget film.[12] Macdonald stated, 'we feel very strongly that we want [the channel] involved. Not so much from the financial point of view (we were offered more money elsewhere) but from a creative point of view'. Channel 4 could offer filmmakers a space for creative freedom, offering advice and support but tending not to interfere too much editorially. Aukin was also concerned with protecting the creative interests of filmmakers – for example, PolyGram (which distributed *Shallow Grave*) had offered to co-finance *Trainspotting*, but only on the condition that one scene be cut from the script: the surreal scene of the film where the main character, Renton, dives into the self-professed 'worst toilet in Scotland' to retrieve his heroin capsules. The team was unhappy about this, and Aukin felt that this scene was integral to the film and that the channel should instead fully finance it for £1.76 million. In Aukin's words, this was 'a clear statement of why Channel 4 can be important to a filmmaker'.[13] This shows that the channel could work to protect the interests of filmmakers in negotiations with other financiers who were concerned with box-office appeal at the expense of distinctiveness. The channel invested significant money to ensure that the creative integrity of the production was kept intact – but this was also a shrewd decision from the channel's perspective.

David Hesmondhalgh argues that for any cultural organisation geared towards commercial success, such as a film studio, 'star symbol creators' – writers, directors, celebrities and products – are well rewarded and publicised as part of a desire to offset risk by branding.[14] For the channel, this idea of 'reward' worked quite literally, on one level. For example, in the late 1990s, following the success of films like *The Madness of King George*, *Shallow Grave*, *Four Weddings* and *Trainspotting*, Film on Four became increasingly important to Channel 4's brand identity. The channel's own emphasis on its activities as a filmmaker and a major force in British film production became far more pronounced. This can be seen particularly in the rhetoric adopted by Michael Grade, who, in 1994, began publicly campaigning for the channel to be released from its obligation to provide ITV with a portion of its revenue as part of a 'safety net' should the channel's advertising profits fall below 14%. In 1997, when the funding agreement was lifted, Grade injected £100 million into Film on Four to be budgeted over the next four years. Individual productions became increasingly important to the channel's corporate image, as did its relationship with directors like Danny Boyle and Damien O'Donnell, as films like *Trainspotting* and *East is East* (1999) came to serve as examples of the channel's edgy, youth-oriented image.

Shallow Grave represented an important cornerstone for a number of reasons. If Grade, Aukin and his team can be believed, the success of the film was influential at the highest level within the structural organisation of the channel, and it was one of a few productions which came to define the image of Film on Four in this era. *Shallow Grave* also gives an insight into how Film on Four changed under Aukin in the 1990s. Film on Four was moving in a new direction, in commissioning a genre film and essentially indicating the channel's interest in broadening the range of the types of films commissioned. Equally, *Shallow Grave* serves as an example of how the channel could provide support to first-time filmmakers by offering advice and suggestions, working with filmmakers at script and production level. Aukin facilitated the collaboration between Boyle, Hodge and Macdonald, working with them on all levels from development to production. The funding decision behind *Trainspotting* also shows that the channel could act in protecting the interests of filmmakers in negotiation with other financiers and provides an example of how Channel 4 worked with filmmakers, not just on a one-off basis, but continually. Though Film on Four became more commercial in this era, this was not an overriding factor and the channel continued to be a space where filmmakers had the freedom to experiment, funding low-budget films within the public service remit of the channel. However, the above case study looks at one film, and is thus too particular to allow for general conclusions about Film on Four's support for new talent from 1982. With this in mind, the following section will look at the channel's short-film strand, Short and Curlies, as a way of examining the effectiveness of Film on Four's initiatives to find new filmmaking talent. This section will also aim to draw some conclusions regarding the importance of relationships in the film industry in terms of how projects come together from idea stage to production.

Talent-finding initiatives: Short and Curlies

In 1987, Channel 4 collaborated on a series of 11-minute short films. From 1987 to 1995 the strand was known as Short and Curlies, and was produced in conjunction with British Screen. However, following a bitter clash with British Screen after its deal with BSkyB to provide the pay-tv rights to most of the films they funded, Channel 4 ended this partnership and decided to produce these short films with the BBC instead, with the strand being renamed Brief Encounters. From 1997 the strand was again renamed, to Jump Cuts, and was fully funded by the channel. The following section will attempt to examine how useful this initiative actually was in providing Film on Four with a new generation of writing and directing talent. It will also argue that talent-finding initiatives were less important to Film on Four than the relationships and contacts they generated, and will move more widely to discuss the importance of informal networks and contacts in the British film industry.

The aim of the 'Short and Curlies' series was to commission writers and directors who were already working in television or the arts who had never been given the opportunity to work on film. The title was taken from Mike Leigh's 19-minute short film *The Short and Curlies*, which was commissioned for the first series. Aside from Leigh's film, it was mandatory that each film should be a directorial debut, and in many cases this was also true for the writers. According to a Channel 4 press release issued before the first series of Short and Curlies was broadcast, some directors had come straight from film school, or were frustrated actors or technicians who were finding it extremely difficult to break into feature-film directing – people like actor Peter Chelsom, animator Mole Hill and documentary filmmaker Sue Clayton.[15]

What was particularly innovative about this series was that rather than being merely 'short films' these productions were envisioned as 'mini-features'. They were to be shot on 35mm, with the filmmakers working in the same conditions as they would if they were making a Film on Four, from feature-film-specific union agreements to production values and script quality.[16] The channel also intended to get distributors interested in screening these short films before main features in cinemas, at a time when screening shorts was uncommon.[17] The cost of these productions was to reflect this 'feature in miniature' aspect of the films, with budgets ranging from £70,000 to £100,000 throughout the life of the series.[18] In the channel's Press Information Packs, the shorts were often referred to as being '11 minute feature film[s]'.[19] The strand was also envisioned by the channel as being 'a parallel to its support of feature films through Film on Four'.[20] The close association with Film on Four shows that the channel was attempting to discover and train new talent by assessing the ability of directors to work within feature-style constraints, with an eye to finding writers and directors who could make the transition to feature-length films.

Rising production costs were an incentive for the channel to produce short films, in order to allow new filmmakers to make their mark. As a means of providing 'calling cards' for young filmmakers, the strand achieved varying degrees of success. Peter Chelsom, Mark Herman and Gurinder Chadha all moved on to their first features after directing their own short films, while writers like Philip Ridley (*The Krays* [Peter Medak, 1990]) moved on to screenplay writing. Gurinder Chadha's first short film, *'I'm British, But . . .'*, was taken up by the BFI's pilot New Directors scheme, and she submitted *Bhaji on the Beach* (1993) on the strength of this. Channel 4 asked her to develop her skills on a Short and Curlies 11-minute film called *A Nice Arrangement*, and Chadha was given the go-ahead for *Bhaji* as the channel was pleased with her work.[21] In 1993 *The Independent* noted that more filmmakers were going down the short-film route. Mark Herman went to Disney after making his short film *Underground Conversation*, subsequently persuading the studio to back *Blame It on the Bellboy* (1992). Following the success of her short film *Heart Songs*, Sue Clayton also made *The Disappearance of Finbar* (1996) for Channel 4.[22]

However, the series was never intended to serve as a creative outlet for relatively inexperienced would-be filmmakers. For example, Clayton was by no means a first-time director. She had made many television dramas and documentaries, and was in talks with Channel 4 to make a feature film prior to the production of her Short and Curlies film.[23] She stated in an interview in 1993:

> It seems ironic that Heart Songs was billed as my first film, because it was actually something like my 17th, but all the others were documentaries or television dramas or whatever. Heart Songs was my first chance to work in 35mm and to think in terms of the depth that features can have – not just depth of character, but depth of image too. It gives you a different sense of place – we shot it all on location in Ontario – and of the relationship of characters to that place.[24]

Even Short and Curlies filmmakers straight out of film school had impressive qualifications. For example, Chris Fallon (*The New Look* [1990]) graduated from the Royal College of Art in 1986, where he wrote and directed student films which achieved success at film festivals in Germany, France, Finland and the USA.

Short and Curlies directors went on to work on subsequent feature films, many of them with Channel 4. However, considering the number of short films produced by the channel between 1987 and 1999, the number of directors making their first feature with the channel was fairly low. In a recent interview, Allon Reich stated that the number of direct moves from the short films to Film on Four was lower than expected. Although 'there was some conversion' it was 'not enough, I don't think'.[25] However, Reich argued that the strand was very valuable in providing experience for filmmakers working in the industry in general: 'There's a few people who learned a lot and moved on, if you look at the crew and production as well.' Furthermore, the short-film strand, though not as significant 'in itself', was extremely important for attracting filmmakers to the Channel 4 offices and developing relationships with young writers and directors as a result.[26] Though the strand did not directly provide much of a talent base for Film on Four, it was, according to Reich, important in that it added to and expanded the network of relationships between the channel and young writers, producers, directors and technicians.

The Channel 4 commissioning process was relatively democratic and unrestricted, at least in theory. However, the department did not have the staff to read every script submitted and often projects arose from other avenues, such as informal contacts. Interestingly, although the commissioning process was intended to provide the department with the bulk of its programming material, according to Karin Bamborough, few films were actually the result of unsolicited scripts.[27] Relationships and informal meetings and discussions were thus as important as established process, if not more so. This method of working is particularly evident in the film industry, and as such one can argue that this informal network of relationships arose from the necessity of working with established film production companies, commissioning products for that industry as well as for television. Furthermore, as the *Shallow Grave* case study illustrates, a commission could simply be the result of being in the right place at the right time.

The importance of being in Soho

Quantifying the success of any film company based on informal networking and chance encounters would be an exercise in counterfactual history as the data required to support such an analysis would be very difficult to find. Thinking through such processes can be seen as counter-productive, but ignoring them equally so, if only because we must recognise that the success of any production company is based on a shrewd business strategy but also on a complex network of relationships and a certain amount of luck. The idea of luck, of simply being in the right place at the right time, is something that is often missing from academic work on the film industry, because this is an extremely difficult idea to couch in academic terms. However, as previous chapters have illustrated via case studies of films like *The Crying Game* (Neil Jordan, 1992), *Shallow Grave* and companies like Working Title, risk, luck and chance meetings with informal contacts are absolutely integral to filmmaking. This idea does need to be qualified somewhat, however. For example, David Aukin's anecdote of being slipped the script for *Shallow Grave* by his driver and then reading it out of boredom on a flight to London is the kind of story that is often told to journalists in hindsight to add to the mystique around an unexpected hit. More often, there are many underlying reasons why films come together in a 'cottage' industry without a stable financial infrastructure. Stephen Woolley's success in drawing together finance for *The Crying Game* was less about chance than dogged persistence, a necessary skill in the arsenal of a film producer.

In the film industry, informal networks often arise from companies and filmmakers working in close proximity to one another – as Ivan Turok in particular notes in his work on creative clusters in film and television.[28] The Channel 4 commissioning process did not in theory necessitate the need for talent and companies to group in a specific location, and therefore the channel did not have a need for a close talent base or 'pool' of resources. However, as interviews with Channel 4 Commissioning Editors reveal, the commissioning process only represented part of the methods through which film projects originated.

Film production companies, large and small, have historically clustered around the Soho area. According to Bahar Dumaz, a geographically clustered network of relationships is essential to the functioning of the British film industry:

> Interviewees see the advantages of Soho in terms of proximity, diversity and a 24/7 city where 'everything co-exists, everybody is here, and everything is happening here'. On the other hand, they also see some disadvantages of Soho as a location, including congestion, high rents, parking and transportation and accommodation issues including ventilation, heating, inflexibility and inadequate space.[29]

Durmaz's research showed that close proximity to bars, cafes and places where informal creative discussions can take place is also important to producers:

> Both Istanbul and London respondents say that the city's cosmopolitan structure and diversity made them feel more creative and inspired. They like to be in touch with other creative people that motivate them. Interviewees say that they like being in the city centre where they have the opportunity to go to cafes, bars, cinemas.[30]

Informal discussions and meetings could potentially provide the basis for long-term projects. For example, it was while Palace's Stephen Woolley was in a tavern in Soho that he overheard Tim Bevan talking about a potential deal with the Dutch banking firm Pierson, Heldring and Pierson. Following this discussion, Woolley set about making a funding deal with the company himself.[31] Furthermore, research has shown that informal networking is important at all levels of film and television production. Research undertaken by Helen Blair in 1999 found that this was essential to technical film workers. For example, interviews with employees working on a film production showed that 54% had heard about their current job informally from friends or family, 17% from contacting companies directly and just 8% from advertisements. Over

half had secured their first ever film or TV job through personal rec-
ommendation.[32] Clusters of companies and talent provide networks of
informal relationships, which lead on to other projects. For David Aukin,
in many ways a mediator between the film and television industries, it was
important to be close to this creative filmmaking centre.

Conclusion

Though Channel 4 gradually became more commercially oriented and
professionalised from the early 1990s, and while many Film on Four
productions were commissioned with an eye to theatrical distribution,
Film on Four continued to enjoy a level of autonomy and economic
protection within the channel. This chapter has also looked at the role
of Film on Four in mediating between the film and television industries,
offering insights into the ways in which David Aukin and his team worked
with filmmakers while negotiating the broadcasting environment. Aukin
could often get involved editorially (he fought to create space for Boyle,
Macdonald and Hodge to realise their ideas) and he could also act to
protect the interests of filmmakers in the face of disagreements with other
co-production partners. This case study also shows how the success of
individual productions like *Shallow Grave* could strengthen the position
of Film on Four within the channel and directly influence policy. Indeed,
this film might be seen as the first in a series of productions which caused
Channel 4 to re-evaluate the importance of its identity as a funder of
British film. Talent-finding initiatives were, however, less important than
the contacts and relationships they generated, with few directors and
writers actually moving on to work on Film on Four productions. In the
final part of this book, we move away from issues of production to look
at the marketing, distribution and exhibition of Films on Four in international markets.

Notes

1. Allon Reich, personal communication, 25 July 2012.
2. *The Independent*, 5 June 1991.
3. David Aukin, 'Farewell to Four', *The Guardian*, 3 November 1997.
4. Allon Reich, personal communication, 25 July 2012.
5. *Ibid.*

6. *The Scotsman*, 20 January 1995.

7. Danny Boyle, quoted in Ronan Bennett, 'Lean, Mean, and Cruel', *Sight and Sound*, 5:1 (January 1995).

8. Amy Raphael, *Danny Boyle: In His Own Words* (London: Faber and Faber, 2011), 56.

9. Adam Dawtrey, 'Screen's Siren Song Lures Brit Legiters', *Variety*, 12–18 December 1994.

10. *Ibid.*

11. *Ibid.*

12. Raphael, *Danny Boyle*, 73.

13. *Interview*, 23 February 2012.

14. David Hesmondhalgh, *The Cultural Industries* (London: Sage, 2002), 58.

15. *Ibid.*

16. Kevin Jackson, 'When Every Second Counts', *The Independent*, 8 February 1993, 12.

17. *Ibid.*

18. *Ibid.*

19. Channel 4 Television, Channel 4 Press Information Packs, 1991, weeks 18, 29.

20. Channel 4 Television, Channel 4 Press Information Packs, 1989/90, weeks 49, 30.

21. Andrea Stuart, 'Blackpool Illumination', *Sight and Sound*, 4:2, February 1994.

22. Jackson, 'When Every Second Counts', 12.

23. *Ibid.*

24. *Ibid.*

25. Allon Reich, personal communication, 25 July 2012.

26. *Ibid.*

27. Karin Bamborough, personal communication, 1 December 2011.

28. Ivan Turok, 'Cities, Clusters and Creative Industries: The Case of Film and Television in Scotland', *European Planning Studies*, 11:5 (2003), 549–65.

29. Bahar Durmaz, Stephen Platt and Tan Yigitcanlar, 'Creativity, Culture Tourism: Istanbul and London Film Industries', *International Journal of Culture, Tourism and Hospitality*, 4:3 (2010), 206.

30. *Ibid.*, 208.

31. Angus Finney, *The Egos Have Landed: The Rise and Fall of Palace Pictures* (London: William Heinemann, 1996), 70.

32. Helen Blair, 'Working in Film: Employment in a Project Based Industry', *Personnel Review*, 30:2 (2001), 180.

Part Four

International Crossings

Chapter 8

Channel 4 in Europe

Across Britain, Europe and the USA, the 1980s and 1990s brought an increase in co-productions, an increase in television funding, the emergence of the art-house/cross-over film and the growth of transnationalism.[1] From its inception film has always been 'transnational' in the sense that distribution and exhibition have, from the earliest days of filmmaking, transcended national boundaries. But in the late 1980s and early 1990s, with a rise in European co-productions, the growth of the independent sector in the USA and the establishment of greater links between the European and American 'indie' sector, assigning fixed identities to national cinemas became increasingly problematic. Any study of the influence of Channel 4 films on British film culture must therefore necessarily account for how these films have travelled and impacted upon other cinemas. As film travels, reception by other nations or parts of the world adds its own particular 'stamp' to a production. As Thomas Elsaesser argues,

> European films intended for one kind of (national) audience … undergo a sea change as they cross the Atlantic, and on coming back, find themselves bearing the stamp of yet another cultural currency. The same is true of some Hollywood films. What the *auteur* theory saw in them was not what the studios or even the directors 'intended', but this did not stop another generation of American viewers appreciating exactly what the *Cahiers du Cinéma* critics had extracted from them.[2]

Channel 4 had a longstanding relationship with European film culture through its film sponsorship practices, while the channel also quickly established a firm presence at European film festivals. Participation in festival competitions brought a valuable element of cultural prestige to the channel (a fact which was continually emphasised in annual reports and press publications), but it also provided an important means of exhibition and exposure for Channel 4-funded films. Through a case study of Ken Loach's *Riff-Raff* (1991), this chapter will examine the importance of the festival circuit as an exhibition outlet for Channel 4 films, as well as a means of facilitating co-production deals.

Film Four International

Channel 4's involvement in supporting European film production is widely thought to have begun with David Rose's agreement to fund the Wim Wenders film *Paris, Texas* in 1984, though the channel was involved in co-productions with other European companies and broadcasters from its beginnings. For example, in 1982 the channel made Pascal Ortega's *Bad Hats* with TF1 Films and Les Productions Audiovisuelles, and in 1984 also co-funded Chris Petit's *Flight to Berlin* with the German Federal Republic. It is true that the Fiction Department's interest in European film intensified throughout the 1980s, in part due to the industrial and economic difficulties discussed earlier in this book. However, it was rare for the channel to offer more than the pre-buying of television rights for a European co-production; for example, both *Paris, Texas* and Andrei Tarkovsky's *The Sacrifice* (1986) were funded in this way. Co-productions could be screened in the Film on Four strand or the Film on Four International strand, which was introduced in 1986 to showcase the channel's involvement with international cinema. Film on Four International was usually used to show productions where the channel had invested small amounts, or completion money, for a production. The Channel 4 Press Information Packs usually make clear that though many of these films received money from the channel at the pre-production stage, they would not generally be considered to be, like Films on Four, produced or co-produced by the channel.

The interest of Film Four International in showcasing and selling films at European markets and film festivals also increased in this era. FFI was created in 1983 as part of Channel 4 International and was responsible for managing the rights to films funded by the channel. It was also responsible for selling those films to domestic and international distributors (where the channel had equity and rights to a production). FFI had only a token stall at Cannes in 1983, but towards the mid-1980s Channel 4's position as a co-producer of foreign films began to be taken more seriously, as did the potential for festivals like Cannes to increase sales of Channel 4-funded films. This had much to do with changes in attitudes at Film Four International. For example, when Carole Meyer took over as head of FFI in 1984, bringing her experience as a former member of the BFI Production Board, she focused more closely on the international sales aspect of the company. In 1986, *Variety* noted that Channel 4 was taking films to Cannes that seemed more mainstream in appeal, like *The Supergrass* (Peter Richardson, 1985), *Heavenly Pursuits* (Charles Gormley, 1986) and *Eat the Peach* (Peter Ormrod, 1986). These films appeared to be aimed at a wider market than a film like *Letter to Brezhnev* (Chris Bernard, 1985). The result was, according to *Variety*, that FFI was gaining more credibility at Cannes than ever before.[3]

In 1986, FFI pitched thirteen films at Cannes, double what it was promoting in 1985. Meyer stated that 'we work on the principle that 50 percent of a picture's budget should be covered by advances'.[4] Ten percent of films screened at the Venice Film Festival in this year also involved Channel 4, with the channel providing the completion money for that year's Golden Lion winner *Sans toit ni loi* (Agnès Varda, 1986).[5] FFI was beginning to realise the importance of the festival circuit to the success of Films on Four in Europe. The sales arm of Channel 4 films would also begin to operate more according to the dictates of the sales and festival circuits. For example, the appropriate festival would be selected for the appropriate film, the film would be entered for selection, and the production would need to be completed in time to be showcased at said festival.[6] Production and post-production deadlines for the slate of films funded by Channel 4 in a given year would be chosen according to the festival calendar. FFI also began to have more of a presence at sales festival MIFED, as well as selecting films at pre-production and production stage to be pre-sold at business festivals like Cannes. Festivals operate as an alternative exhibition network for films which might not be seen elsewhere, and serve as exhibition outlets and launch pads for new talent.[7] They also facilitate relationships between film financiers and filmmakers, and, because of the international dimension, they can attract international investors, leading to co-productions.[8]

Riff-Raff and the importance of the European film festival circuit

The success of Channel 4 films on the European festival circuit not only widened the appeal of British film to a European audience, but also gained greater recognition for, and changed perceptions of, British film at home.

Drawing upon Pierre Bourdieu's concept of symbolic capital and utilising the work of Thomas Elsaesser and Marijke de Valck on the 'value adding process'[9] inherent in the international film festival circuit, this case study will focus on Ken Loach's *Riff-Raff*, a low-budget, made-for-television film which secured distribution in the UK only after it had won the FIPRESCI prize at Cannes in 1991.[10] It will also examine how cultural consecration through 'value addition' changed perspectives towards *Riff-Raff* at home and abroad, charting the transformation of a small-scale film for television into a widely acclaimed art-house hit, while also analysing the ways in which that transformation highlighted serious inefficiencies in the British film industry. Lastly, this study will look more broadly at the performance of Loach's films in Europe and will argue that the festival circuit has been essential to the international success of his productions and of Films on Four in general.

Film festivals are not insular – they operate within a complex global network which is hierarchically divided. The influence of a festival depends on its status. There are 'A', or top-rated, festivals (Cannes, Venice, Berlin) and 'B', second-rated festivals (this is regulated by the Paris-based organisation, the International Federation of Film Producers Associations, or FIAPF).[11] Festivals compete with each other for key dates, films and audiences, but they also compete along the same axes; they resemble each other in their internal organisation, while differentiating themselves in terms of their programming and the image they seek to present. FIAPF must also ensure that each festival sequentially follows the other in the festival calendar, allowing filmmakers and journalists to travel the circuit.[12] This chapter cannot attempt to do justice to the complexities of the international film festival network and the subtle hierarchies within it, but these studies have been comprehensively undertaken elsewhere. Rather, for the purposes of this study, it is important to note the role that film festivals play in consecrating elements such as authorship, production, distribution, exhibition and cultural prestige. Elsaesser argues that one of their key functions is to 'categorize, classify, sort and sift the world's annual film-production . . . supporting, selecting, celebrating and rewarding – in short, [by] adding value and cultural capital'.[13] The festival network is thus a key power-grid in the global film industry, affecting production, distribution, exhibition and taste.

An important aspect of the circuit is 'value addition'. A film can gain cultural value in the form of awards at a festival, and this can translate into economic value via distribution deals. Films can gain further symbolic capital as they travel along the circuit, achieving something like a 'snowball' effect. Valck argues that the value-adding process at a festival is characterised through three phases – selection, awards and mediation. Films are selected for the festival by the festival director and/or a committee. Some films compete with each other for awards, and the winners are chosen by a jury, whose decisions will naturally be subject to the 'buzz' and press attention created around that film during the festival. The third phase of value addition involves the cultural prestige bestowed on a film at a festival entering media discourse around the world – thus festival value is translated into media value, and this in turn can potentially be translated into economic value through distribution deals, video and DVD deals. At film festivals, then, productions accumulate symbolic capital in the form of publicity, prizes and attention which can lead to widespread media awareness and economic gain, and this, as Elsaesser puts it, is 'life and death' to a film.[14]

Riff-Raff unexpectedly won a major award at an 'A' festival, Cannes, and this brought cultural prestige which generated media attention, awards and distribution deals that might otherwise have been difficult to obtain. Throughout the 1970s and 80s, Loach had difficulty attracting finance for his projects (with the exception of his 1986 film *Fatherland*, an international production set both in Germany and the UK and co-funded by Channel 4). However, his career really took off in the 1990s with the international success of films like *Hidden Agenda* (1990), *Riff-Raff, Raining Stones* (1993), *Ladybird, Ladybird* (1994) and *Land and Freedom* (1995). This success was in large part due to an ongoing relationship with Channel 4 and the forging of new relationships with writers like Jim Allen and Bill Jesse. Loach's partnerships with producers Sally Hibbin and Rebecca O'Brien of Parallax Pictures were also a major factor in raising his profile in this era.[15] *Riff-Raff* was a collaboration between Loach and Bill Jesse which had started life at Columbia but later moved to Channel 4.[16] The film follows the story of Stevie, a Glaswegian construction worker, and his experiences working on a construction site in London building a block of luxury flats. In characteristic Loach style, the film relies partly on dramatic realism, partly on improvisation, and critiques the worst excesses of Thatcherism while also lamenting the lack of political mobilisation within the British working classes. Following the film's completion, it was refused by every UK distributor but given a short run at the National Film Theatre, where it opened to favourable reviews. Anthony Hayward states that it was producer Sally Hibbin who made an international success of the film after this disappointing start:

> We showed it to British distributors and had quite a bad reception. One of them stomped out and said he had had enough of British realism. Then we were invited to the Directors Fortnight at the 1991 Cannes film festival. Channel 4 said they could not afford to send us there because they believed it wouldn't sell. So I told their head of drama, David Aukin, that we had some money left in the budget and asked if we could spend it on getting to Cannes. He said yes, we went and the film received the most extraordinary standing ovation.[17]

At the festival the film took the International Critics' Prize. Following this award, *Riff-Raff* gained subsequent accolades at smaller festivals and eventually won Best Film at the European Film Awards of that year, gradually accumulating symbolic value which resulted in distribution deals in countries like France, Germany, Sweden and Finland.[18] After it had sold around Europe, Palace Pictures (which had initially turned the film down) decided to release it, although it was too late by this point for the film to achieve its full potential.[19]

The 'buzz' surrounding the film at Cannes in May 1991 generated debate among the media at home. Press discourse predominantly expressed bafflement at the lack of recognition for *Riff-Raff* in the UK and saw the attention the film garnered in Europe as indicative of problems within the British film industry. Simon Hattenstone of *The Guardian* stated:

> Ken Loach must be a confused man. His Channel 4 comedy *Riff-Raff* was shown at the National Film Theatre, but no distributor was interested in giving it a wider cinema release. Too small-scale, they said. Why pay to watch a story about exploitation of working-class builders when you could be wallowing in another E. M. Forster adaptation? Who would understand all those strange dialects anyway? Well, much of the world, it turns out. Off it went to Cannes, won itself an award and was snapped up by the Germans, Spanish, Italians, French, Israelis and Australians. Astonishingly, even the British have now decided it's worth showing – *Riff-Raff* has been picked up by Palace Pictures for a national release. But why did we have to wait till now?[20]

Shortly after receiving the European Film Award, *Riff-Raff* was showing in thirty cinemas in Germany and seventeen in France, while there were only three prints available in the whole of the UK before Palace decided to release it in the light of its European success. This was evidence, as one commentator noted, 'that it's now well-nigh impossible to find a place in the UK market for even a very good British film'.[21] Lack of appreciation for British film at home was a frequent lament of film critics, but this intensified as a result of the international attention surrounding the film. Other critics noted a natural prejudice towards low-budget features on the part of UK distributors. On 18 April 1991 Derek Malcolm reported that *Riff-Raff* would shortly be shown at Cannes, where 'there isn't much doubt that it will *be treated as film rather than jumped-up television*' (my emphasis).[22] After entry into the festival, *Riff-Raff* arguably lost its baggage as a realist drama funded by a broadcaster – by dint of its very selection at the festival gates it automatically became a film by a director already considered an auteur in France.

The failure to distribute the film in the UK had a significant effect on Channel 4, causing executives to re-evaluate the viability of funding films for theatrical release at a time of great uncertainty in the British broadcasting environment.[23] Theatrical release had always been a problem, with many Films on Four receiving very limited art-house distribution. But *Riff-Raff* was released in the early 1990s, which was, as has been noted, an economically inopportune moment for the channel. David Aukin stated in a press interview:

> We made a decent movie in Ken Loach's *Riff-Raff* but we couldn't get proper exhibition or distribution for it … so you begin to think, why bother to make films for cinemas at all? Why not make films for TV and cut out the cinemas? If we can't get our films decently distributed, the pressure on me to do so will be enormous. It would be a reversal of Film on 4 policy. But nothing is forever.[24]

Aukin decided that theatrical release would remain a staple of Film on Four's output. But the fact that Channel 4 films had consistently proven that they could be more successful abroad than in the UK remained a source of frustration. The channel's Chief Executive Michael Grade spoke at the premiere of Peter Chelsom's *Hear My Song* (which also had trouble gaining distribution in the UK) in 1992 and stated that the channel was 'fed up with being at the mercy of UK distributors after films are completed' and lamented the fact that *Riff-Raff* had 'been seen by more people in French cinemas than in British'.[25]

Reliance on festivals and specialised distribution in Europe has also gained Loach a reputation in Britain as being an 'art' director, even though this label has not always been reflective of the content of his work. John Hill argues that Loach's films have become 'art' cinema in the UK in part because of the legitimacy conferred by European film festivals and specialised international distribution.[26] Steve Neale argues that European art cinema relies on certain conventions, its main features being a suppression of action, stress on character and 'a foregrounding of style and authorial enunciation'.[27] However, this is not typical of Loach's work. Rather, he tends to eschew showy stylistic techniques and has always denied that he is an 'artsy' director. Like many of his works, *Riff-Raff* relies on genre elements like comedy. It was made using actors with real-life experience, was shot in chronological order and semi-observational in style, using techniques partly drawn from documentary and classical modes. The auteur is also central to art cinema, and Loach has always been considered an auteur in Europe (though he frequently denies the label, continually emphasising the collective nature of his work). Yet because of his reliance on film festivals like Cannes (which privileges the auteur) and distribution on European art circuits, his productions have always been marketed in Europe as 'Ken Loach films'.[28] Rather than aesthetic considerations, festival prestige and modes of distribution in Europe have largely determined the cultural status of Loach's films in the UK.

Loach's films have suffered from a lack of distribution in Britain but have usually managed to make at least some money for two reasons: their low budgets and their viability in international markets. As difficult as it has been to penetrate the industry, European recognition through

Figure 8.1   Ken Loach's *Riff-Raff.*

awards gained at festivals has raised the profile of the director and his films in the UK. More generally, the cultural capital accumulated through the festival network has been essential to the success of many other Channel 4-funded films. Where it has been difficult to obtain widespread distribution in the UK, film festivals have been important as an international site of exhibition, as a means of generating prestige and validation for the broadcaster's film-funding practices, and as a way of boosting the profile of British film abroad. As well as *Riff-Raff*, other British films that can be characterised as 'local' such as Michael Radford's *Another Time, Another Place* (1983), Charles Gormley's *Heavenly Pursuits*, Neil Jordan's *Mona Lisa* (1986), Stephen Frears's *Prick Up Your Ears* (1987), David Leland's *Wish You Were Here* (1987) and Terence Davies' *Distant Voices, Still Lives* (1988) have all accumulated significant cultural capital in the form of awards at festivals from Cannes to Locarno and Bergamo to Berlin.

Conclusion

Channel 4 raised the profile of British film in Europe through its participation in film festivals, but this effect was reciprocal – the profile of British film could also be boosted in the UK through the value-adding process inherent in the international film festival circuit. *Riff-Raff* provides an example of a film which suffered from a lack of interest at home but won substantial acclaim in Europe as a result of its participation in a high-profile festival, which in turn led to recognition in the UK (however limited). *Riff-Raff* achieved widespread success in Europe through the value-adding process– the FIPRESCI prize imbued the film with significant cultural capital, the first stage in a cumulative process which translated into distribution deals in countries around the world and culminated in it winning Best Film at the European Film Awards. The success of *Riff-Raff* highlighted problems inherent in the British film industry, but also the fact that low-budget, socially conscious British films, while struggling to achieve distribution in the UK, could achieve significant success abroad. For Loach's films, and for Channel 4 films in general, the festival circuit was key to that success. At the same time, the burgeoning independent sector in the USA was bringing further opportunities, and the channel's partnership with American indie companies like Miramax throughout the 1990s would truly bring Channel 4 films into larger international markets.

Notes

1. Rosalind Galt, *The New European Cinema: Redrawing the Map* (New York: Columbia University Press, 2006), 2.
2. Thomas Elsaesser, *European Cinema: Face to Face with Hollywood* (Amsterdam: Amsterdam University Press, 2005), 46.
3. *Variety*, 11 June 1986.
4. *Ibid.*
5. *Stills* (December/January 1986).
6. Kate Robinson, personal communication, 18 September 2012.
7. Marijke de Valck, *Film Festivals: From European Geopolitics to Global Cinephilia* (Amsterdam: Amsterdam University Press, 2007), 106.
8. *Ibid.*
9. Elseasser, *European Cinema*; Valck, *Film Festivals*.
10. *Screen International*, 6 March 1992.
11. Joseph Lampel, 'Classics Foretold? Contemporaneous and Retrospective Consecration in the UK Film Industry' *Cultural Trends*, 18:3 (2009), 3.
12. Elsaesser, *European Cinema*, 86.
13. Lampel, 'Classics Foretold?', 3.
14. Elsaesser, *European Cinema*, 97.
15. Graham Fuller, *Loach on Loach* (London: Faber and Faber, 1998), 78.
16. Anthony Hayward, *Which Side Are You On? Ken Loach and his Films* (London: Bloomsbury, 2004), 211.
17. *Ibid.*, 214.
18. *Ibid.*
19. *The Guardian*, 3 December 1991.
20. *The Guardian*, 30 May 1991.
21. *The Independent*, 6 December 1991.
22. *The Guardian*, 18 April 1991.
23. BFI Special Collections, Papers of Roger Graef, CF Paper 312, 'Film on Four' (1985).
24. *The Independent*, 5 June 1991.
25. *Television Week*, 5–11 March 1992.
26. John Hill, *Ken Loach: The Politics of Film and Television* (London: Wallflower, 2006), 168.
27. *Ibid.*
28. *Ibid.*, 171.

Chapter 9

Channel 4 and Indiewood

In the 1980s, independent companies were beginning to build an identity in the USA, and many of the films they distributed were British and European. Hector Babenco's *Kiss of the Spider Woman* (1985) grossed $17 million for Island, *A Room with a View* (James Ivory, 1985) grossed $23 million for Cinecom, while *Sid and Nancy* (Alex Cox, 1986) and the Channel 4-funded films *My Beautiful Laundrette* (Stephen Frears, 1985) and *Mona Lisa* (Neil Jordan, 1986) also enjoyed strong box-office earnings.[1] Martin Dale notes roughly three types of indie distributors in the USA in the early 1990s: Mini Majors – larger distributors with an eye to the 'cross-over' market, like New Line, Miramax and Gramercy (set up in a joint venture between PolyGram and Universal in 1993); Classic Indies, which comprised the core of the art-house market, typically releasing on around 400–500 screens, and making up around 3% of the market; and Micro-Indies, companies which would release on a tiny number of screens and expect to gross around $0.5 million per picture. There were between fifteen and twenty of these companies, usually with close links to the festival circuit.[2] Dale also notes a shift in foreign sales, which were once dominated by Europe, particularly by France and Italy, but which by the early 1990s began to revolve mainly around the American independent market. In the early 1990s, the USA provided around 120 new films for sale per year, while Britain provided around thirty, France fifty-five, and others around fifteen to twenty.[3] In terms of buyers for US product, 59% of sales were made in Europe and 35% in Asia. Buyers could vary from national majors, mini-majors (niche, cross-over) and small, prestige art-house distributors. Large US majors tended to keep foreign rights, whereas before 'empire building' they had tended to sell them.[4]

Sarah Street notes that the key to the success of British films in the USA has been effective distribution. In some cases, distribution in North America has also been the key to the success of films on UK cinema circuits. *The Crying Game*, which did extremely well in the USA after failing to draw in audiences in Britain, set a precedent for producers, who realised that it might be more advantageous to release films in the USA first, as American successes might influence UK audiences. For this reason, *The Madness of King George* (Nicholas Hytner, 1994) and *Four Weddings and a Funeral* (Mike Newell, 1994) both opened in America before being released domestically. Relationships with American companies, the aggressive marketing techniques of Miramax and increased recognition of the value of the US festival circuit for launching independent films all contributed to the success of British films in the USA in the 1990s. Festivals like Sundance, Cannes, Venice, Toronto, New York and London were used to build vital press coverage for a film. However, US majors rarely capitalised upon the festival circuit, preferring to focus on the most important event of the film year – the Academy Award ceremonies in March.[5]

The rise of Miramax was almost synonymous with the rise of the American independent sector, and this company had a longstanding relationship with Channel 4 throughout the 1990s. Miramax picked up many Film on Four titles for American distribution and even entered into co-productions with the channel. For example, *True Blue* (Ferdinand Fairfax, 1996) and *The Woodlanders* (Phil Agland, 1997) were picked up by Miramax at Cannes for North American distribution, while Miramax and Channel 4 co-funded Michael Winterbottom's *Sarajevo* (1997) and Todd Haynes's *Velvet Goldmine* (1998). Miramax also picked up *Trainspotting* (Danny Boyle, 1996) and *East is East* (Damien O'Donnell, 1999) for distribution, to varying degrees of success. The following case study will look at Miramax's distribution of *The Crying Game* (Neil Jordan, 1992) in North America in order to offer some insights into the marketing and reception of Films on Four abroad, and the 'sea change' these films can undergo as they cross the Atlantic and come back, as Elsaesser argues, 'bearing the stamp of yet another cultural currency'.[6]

Marketing *The Crying Game* in the UK and the USA

Prior to the international success of films like *Four Weddings and a Funeral*, *The Madness of King George* and *Trainspotting*, *The Crying Game* was Film on Four's first truly global hit. While the growing international appeal of Films on Four in the 1990s had much to do with the editorial decisions of David Aukin in funding a greater variety of product, the establishment of relationships with growing production and distribution outfits like

PolyGram Filmed Entertainment and Miramax was also crucial. Though Miramax was becoming a contender in the American independent market by the late 1980s, *The Crying Game* afforded the company a major breakthrough success, a success which had a significant impact on the growth of the independent sector in the USA and gained the company an important foothold in Europe. This case study will examine how *The Crying Game*, through Miramax's distinctive marketing techniques, was transformed from a low-budget British film part-funded by television into a sensationalist thriller appreciated by American audiences for both its distinctive artistic merit and its controversial marketing campaign. An analysis of the critical reception of *The Crying Game* in North America also reveals how, as one of the first globally successful indie art-house/cross-over productions, the film not only helped to define low-budget British cinema for American audiences but also came to represent a direct challenge to the global cultural hegemony of Hollywood.

Miramax

Miramax[7] was initially inspired by the business practices of British company Palace in its marketing and distribution of films such as *The Evil Dead* (Sam Raimi, 1981) and *Diva* (Jean-Jacques Beineix, 1981) and sought to emulate Palace's approach. The US company would typically acquire cheap, low-budget British and European films which had a certain cultural prestige and re-package these for American audiences.[8] In the late 1980s Miramax gradually moved from acquiring foreign films to making low-budget co-productions. The company sought to trade on its cultural cachet, working to accumulate a library of specialist titles by well-known directors, thereby endearing them to critics, niche audiences and art-house exhibitors.[9] Miramax sought to make commercial films with elements of exploitation but at the same time their aim was to garner some measure of cultural and artistic respectability, walking the fine line between cultural integrity and commercial success.[10] The company would actively find a market for art-house films, and if there was no market they would aim to create one using targeted advertising campaigns. For filmmaking, Miramax would come to typify what Bourdieu argues in *The Field of Cultural Production*, that the 'ideology of creation, which makes the author the first and last source of the value of his creation' serves to hide the fact that the businessman has to exploit this 'sacred' work by finding a market for it and by bringing it to the public, thus consecrating 'a product which he has "discovered" and which would otherwise remain a natural resource'.[11]

The company had its first major success with Steven Soderbergh's *sex, lies, and videotape* in 1989. The film won the *Palme d'or* at Cannes and went on to gross $25 million in the USA, the highest-grossing indie picture in box-office history.[12] Miramax continued to shatter the indie ceiling with the success of *The Crying Game* (which took $63 million) and later with Quentin Tarantino's *Pulp Fiction* (which took $100 million in 1994). With *sex, lies, and videotape*, Miramax extended a strategy that it had used on the Palace co-production *Scandal* (Michael Caton-Jones, 1989). The company heavily emphasised the 'sex' aspect in its marketing campaign and, after screening the production in a limited number of art-house cinemas, gradually widened its release to around 500–600 screens, many of which did not usually show art-house films.[13] John Berra argues that *sex, lies, and videotape* fully established the characteristic Miramax formula: acquiring a film by an established filmmaker or by a rising talent, exposing it at a festival and giving it a limited distribution aimed at smaller, niche markets followed by a wider release and gradual cross-over into the mainstream market.[14] The company also sought to boost the profile of its films through opportunistic publicity stunts cleverly engineered for maximum impact, as it could not afford to spend the money needed for the kinds of saturation marketing campaigns run by the major studios. For example, Christine Keeler was asked to accompany lead actress Joanne Whalley-Kilmer on the interview circuit when promoting *Scandal*, while the company also pressured Daniel Day-Lewis to testify in congress about his role as a cerebral palsy sufferer in *My Left Foot* (Jim Sheridan, 1989) on behalf of the Americans with Disabilities Act (1990).[15]

Following this bold beginning, Miramax faced a series of flops in 1991–2, with films like *Close to Eden* (Nikita Mikhalkov, 1991), *Map of the Human Heart* (Vincent Ward, 1992) and *Tom and Jerry: The Movie* (Phil Roman, 1992). There were also rumours that the company was facing a cash crisis, rumours which were given further fuel when it accepted a cash advance of $5 million from Rank in 1992.[16] *The Crying Game* pulled the company back from the brink, and its unprecedented success was influential in bringing Miramax to the attention of Disney. The company was sold to Disney in 1993 for $80 million, and began operations as the subsidiary of a major studio with the autonomy to greenlight any film up to the amount of $12 million. Miramax is widely credited with the creation of 'Indiewood', a term that became common in the mid-1990s. It denoted a company seen to be somewhere between a small independent and a major studio, or the subsidiary of major studio created for the purpose of producing less commercial films (such as Fox Searchlight, or Sony Pictures Classics).[17] James English suggests that by acquiring growing independent companies as subsidiaries, major studios sought to buy into the cultural currency of the independents, seeking to be involved with work that was seen as challenging in order to appeal to audiences which sought to define themselves against more mainstream Hollywood fare. Such companies could be characterised positively, as existing at the edges of Hollywood, or negatively, as selling out to the studios. However, John Berra argues that even though Miramax operated under a major studio, it continued to trade on its outsider 'indie' status while also effectively being part of the system.[18]

Following the production of *The Crying Game*, Stephen Woolley and Nik Powell decided to screen the film to the larger indie studios before offering it to smaller art-house distributors, and Miramax picked up the film for £1.5 million, buying out other investors in order to 'expand into a thousand theatres' and keep the profits if the film was successful.[19] Channel 4 agreed to be bought out, but added a 'kicker' to the deal which meant that if the film grossed a certain amount (in this case, $50 million) the channel would receive its share in accordance with its equity investment.[20] In the USA *The Crying Game* first appeared at the Telluride Film Festival in October 1992 to rave reviews.[21] Miramax engineered a marketing campaign which followed their by now well-established pattern of securing press notoriety around the film's release. As it had done with *sex, lies, and videotape*, the company emphasised the thriller aspects in their promotion of the film, with posters using a noir-esque image of Miranda Richardson with her blunt bob as the femme fatale, holding a smoking gun against a black background (it was, interestingly, similar to the 1994 posters for Quentin Tarantino's *Pulp Fiction*). The crux of the campaign revolved around audiences keeping the 'secret' of the protagonist Dil's identity as a transgender woman, an especially problematic campaign for the ways in which it aggressively objectified one of the film's leading protagonists and reduced their gender identity in the film to the status of a 'gimmick' in promotional materials. At Telluride and at subsequent festival and media screenings, Miramax emphatically asked the press not to give away the plot 'twist', a request which the US critics almost unanimously received with enthusiasm. The need to keep the 'secret' was impressed upon the audience by the critics and by the publicity for the film, which used the tagline 'the movie everyone is watching, but nobody is giving away its secrets'.[22] According to telephone research carried out by the company, 75% of the audience was still unaware of the 'twist' by February 1993.[23]

James English suggests that Academy Awards are the best instruments for converting cultural prestige into capital,[24] and this was certainly the case following *The Crying Game*'s six Oscar nominations. Miramax strategically increased the number of screens on which the film was showing from 255 to 735, with Miramax SVP Gerry Rich stating that 'the numbers show that Oscar nominations made the movie very accessible for a mainstream audience'.[25] There was already a 'buzz' about *The Crying Game*, which had been showing for thirteen weeks and had sold out in many theatres, but the Oscar nominations undoubtedly fanned this popularity and were a key factor in bringing the film to the attention of the US filmmaking establishment.

The film had been released earlier in the UK, to generally good reviews.[26] Many critics decided not to spoil the so-called 'twist' upon the film's release, but a few decided not to engage with the glibly conspiratorial marketing campaign. Nigel Andrews of the *Financial Times* wrote a lukewarm review in which he stated that 'an initially chaste romance

Figure 9.1 Miranda Richardson as a film-noir-esque femme fatale in *The Crying Game*.

begins, disturbed only when the girlfriend (Jaye Davidson) is revealed to be no girl at all'.[27] *The Crying Game* was first released by Mayfair in the UK, where it took just £2 million. The film re-opened after it had received the Academy Award nominations and taken over $50 million at the US box office. Its reception in the UK had much to do with the timing and subject matter of the film, since it was released at a time when the IRA was stepping up its mainland campaign. The *Daily Telegraph* noted that

> the recent plague of bombs in London will, no doubt, make it harder than usual for British cinema goers to accept the notion of an IRA man with a conscience turned too delicate for the dirty work of terrorism. That, however, is what *The Crying Game* requires us to swallow as its initial premise.[28]

In addition, Stephen Rea's much publicised relationship with former IRA activist Dolours Price may also have affected the popularity of the film. In 1973, the Price sisters were arrested for their part in the car bombings which took place outside the Old Bailey and injured 170 people.[29]

Palace criticised distributor Mayfair for failing to do justice to the film in its marketing campaign.[30] Woolley also penned indictments of British film critics for refusing to embrace British product, stating that although it had been well received in the USA, 'no one would write about *The Crying Game* here. As soon as they knew it was about Ireland and mentioned the IRA, they said "forget it"'.[31] Furthermore, the fact that the film was not nominated in the *Evening Standard* Film Awards, despite being partly shot in London, made Woolley feel like he was being 'totally snubbed' by the establishment.[32] Palace's reputation in Wardour Street may also have been a factor, in terms of the company's tendency to attract criticism due to its apparently haphazard management style.

While a major factor in *The Crying Game*'s success, it is worth considering how far Miramax's marketing gimmick contributed to the profile of the film in the USA. The complicity of the press in keeping the 'secret' was essential in raising considerable critical awareness across hundreds of US publications. The *New Yorker* called the film 'an amazing new movie' which halfway through revealed 'a huge, jaw-dropping surprise – a revelation that changes utterly our understanding of everything that has gone before'.[33] The *LA Daily News* called Jordan's script 'an extraordinary puzzle piece, and its nature precludes me from revealing key plot developments here (if anybody who sees the movie before you do starts talking about it, immediately cover your ears)'.[34]

However, reviewers also emphasised that the marketing gimmick was not the only reason to see the movie, as 'the big shock is much more than a narrative trick' but rather 'a daring, poetic imagining of what it means never to feel the same about anything again'.[35] Comparisons were drawn between *The Crying Game* and Jordan's earlier work, with the director very much celebrated as an auteur director.

The first half of the film is set in Ireland, and recalls the eerie rural stillness and subtle surrealism of *Angel* (1982), dealing as it does with politics but also with more universal themes of love, mortality and vengeance. As Fergus (Stephen Rea) tentatively bonds with IRA captive Jody (Forest Whitaker), Jordan weaves in an overall premise questioning the justification of violence and the nature of revenge at the expense of Fergus's own humanity. The second part of the film, set in London, offers a stark contrast, as Fergus is drawn into a relationship with Dil, Jody's ex-lover. Set in a seedy underworld of smoky nightclubs, dilapidated high-rise flats and darkened, rain-lashed streets, the film recalls the noir aesthetic of *Mona Lisa* (Neil Jordan, 1986), with Jaye Davidson playing the role of a femme fatale alongside Miranda Richardson. The film then escalates into a tense political thriller while Fergus struggles to come to terms with his sexuality and subverted gender expectations. The revelation of Dil as transgender was admired for the way it sought to make viewers actively identify with and question the themes of the film, imbuing the narrative with a level of complexity that encouraged audiences to re-evaluate ideas about masculinity, queer identity, sexuality and gender. The *New York Times* asserted that 'what makes the film startling, according to numerous critics, is not only its unexpected twists of plot . . . but also its exploration of the blurred nature of love, trust and compassion and the unpredictability of human emotion'.[36]

The Crying Game's stylistic idiosyncrasies were explicitly celebrated against the apparent creative blandness of recent studio product. The *Orange County Register* noted that 'there's no doubt that *The Crying Game* could never have survived the diluting influence of the American studio system. Everything that's exciting and surprising and meaningful about it would have been "polished" right out by today's formula driven development process.'[37] In *Entertainment Weekly*, Jordan asserted that he was glad that the film had been unable to attract studio finance, as the studios

> would have tried to explain away the political background. They would have tried to soften the racial tension. And they would have

> demanded that the part of Dil be changed in any number of ways.
> And those different, difficult elements are what make people go see
> the movie.[38]

Jordan's more commercial efforts (*High Spirits* [1988], *We're No Angels* [1989]) were also frequently referenced but dismissed out of hand as being studio failures. And if the success of *The Crying Game* exposed the extent to which Hollywood imposes viewer expectations, the validation of the film through its six Academy Award nominations was taken as a sign of the rising independent sector jostling for room in a Hollywood-dominated industry.

British films were well represented at the 1993 Academy Awards – Mike Newell's *Enchanted April* (1991) and Merchant Ivory's *Howards End* (1992, one-fifth financed by Channel 4, which bought the television rights) also received several nominations. However, they were seen by critics less as British films and more as 'indie' films, with their overwhelming presence at the awards in some cases elevated to the status of a *coup*. Some critics speculated about the change behind this turn of events, questioning whether the Academy was trying to send a 'message' to Hollywood.[39] *Howards End, Enchanted April* and *The Crying Game* represented an alternative to the usual studio fare. While *Howards End* might be seen as appealing to traditional American tastes in British heritage cinema, *The Crying Game*, a downbeat noir IRA thriller featuring a transgender protagonist, seemed like a breath of fresh air. It might be possible to view the breakout success and cultural validation of *The Crying Game* by the Academy as symptomatic of wider trends in the American film industry at this time. One reviewer noted that the Academy seemed to have voted against 'the tyranny of the box office', as none of the films nominated had grossed over $100 million in 1992. In the run-up to the awards, 5,000 makers and marketers of film were typically selected to vote (anonymously) for the films to be nominated for that year. There was a feeling that those filmmakers had 'scorned a system whereby a new release has to be a hit in its first weekend or find itself consigned to an early video grave'.[40] The independent sector had carved out an identity in the 1980s and, buoyed by Miramax's breakout success, was beginning to establish itself in the early 1990s. By selecting independent films, the Academy was perceived to be embracing the growing indie sector and breaking the stranglehold of Hollywood dominance.

John Berra asserts that in the UK, art and commerce tend not to meet (with the work of filmmakers like Ken Loach and Mike Leigh widely seen as being elitist), whereas the situation in the US independent sector is quite different.[41] Indeed, as John Hill has argued, a combination of factors, such as the Hollywood domination of UK distribution, limited releases on independent circuits and the association of many smaller independent films with European festivals and auteur culture, has meant that such work has had difficulty garnering broad appeal in the UK. Charles Morris, owner of the Rex, a small private cinema, argued in *The Guardian* that despite the plugs of reviewers like Derek Malcolm for British films, the cinema still found it extremely difficult to bring in customers. A one-night screening of *The Crying Game* in December 1992 attracted just 47 patrons, although Mr Morris noted that 'it was a different story once the Oscar nominations were announced'.[42] The popularity of *The Crying Game* in the USA bought the film commercial validation which in turn made it more popular for British audiences. The film had travelled to the USA as a low-budget, television-funded film (not unlike other low-budget British films given a limited release in the UK market at this time, such as Hanif Kureishi's *London Kills Me* [1991] and David Attwood's *Wild West* [1992]). Due to a combination of unconventional and targeted marketing, timing, box-office receipts, media publicity and Oscar nominations, the film travelled back with a new, more commercial image. *The Crying Game* thus became defined as a significant title in British cinema only by its international success. For British producers and distributors, the film highlighted the prudence of initially releasing a film not in its home market, but in the USA.[43]

The importance of Academy Awards

Oscar nominations were also good publicity for the channel. At the 1993 Academy Awards, Channel 4-funded films won four Oscars, as well as one for best documentary feature. Andrew Higson notes the importance of Oscars in that the validation of such a prestigious award can spill over into the national base. Academy Awards are often much celebrated by the British press, as evidenced by the overwhelming media coverage of films like *Chariots of Fire* (Hugh Hudson, 1981), *Shakespeare in Love* (John Madden, 1998) and *The King's Speech* (Tom Hooper, 2010).[44] A similar celebration can be identified in the press surrounding the 1993 Academy Awards, although it is interesting to note that a large proportion of column space focused mainly on Emma Thompson's nomination and subsequent award for Best Actress in *Howards End. Enchanted April* and *The Crying Game* received Oscar coverage but were usually sidelined towards the bottom of articles, positioned underneath large photographs of Thompson (and husband Kenneth Branagh). It is simply interesting to note that the British film most celebrated was the type of glossy film most exported and consumed by US audiences, and, according to Higson, the most likely to rely on sumptuous *mise en scène* at the expense of engaging with aspects of British political and social life. This suggests that in celebrating the popularity of British film abroad, UK commentators tend (as Nick James has also argued)[45] to defer to perceived American notions of Britishness despite the fact that *The Crying Game* was much publicised across American media outlets.

However, it also appeared that even positive publicity could be too much of a good thing. *The Crying Game* received its first television transmission on Channel 4 in October 1994, and a study of the film's British reception prior to its television release yields interesting results. Far from welcoming the US success of the film, critics were almost unanimously disparaging, with the film receiving worse reviews than it had upon its initial UK release. If the criticisms are taken at face value, displeasure seemed to centre around the US marketing campaign, which had been extremely prominent in both UK and US media, and played heavily on the film's so-called plot twist. In the television listings of *The Sunday Times*, George Perry reviewed the film as 'a tense psychological thriller [which] is supplanted by a silly love story with a notorious twist, and Miranda Richardson as a ruthless IRA terrorist is way over the top'.[46] The *Daily Telegraph* said that 'most critics cried with rapture at this low budget hit drama ... it's controversial, more than a little nasty, the central gimmick is ludicrous and it's also one of the most overrated movies in years. Can critics really be wrong? Judge for yourself'[47] while *The Independent* called it 'overrated'.[48] The controversial political subject matter was also revisited, with a reviewer from the *Financial Times* provocatively suggesting that the film only did so well in the USA because of American ignorance of the political situation in the UK and Ireland: 'Americans confuse America's fight for independence with the activities of Irish terrorists so that the IRA becomes a right-on organisation on their side of the Atlantic.'[49] While Hollywood's stamp of approval may have boosted the box-office popularity of the film in the UK on its re-release (and netted viewing figures of 8 million for its Channel 4 premiere), the reaction of the critical establishment appeared downbeat, with the film regarded as being too heavily publicised and almost too mainstream (strangely, for a television-funded film about the IRA).

The year 1997 also saw a record British representation at the Oscars, as four of the five films nominated in the Best Picture category were made by small independents, and three of the four – *Secrets and Lies* (Mike Leigh, 1996), *The English Patient* (Anthony Minghella, 1996) and *Shine* (Scott Hicks, 1996) – were British films. An article in *The Observer* stated that the Awards had left Hollywood with a 'bloody nose', while Working Title producer Eric Fellner professed the studios to be 'horrified' by the whole affair. When asked to give a reason for their popularity, David Aukin said that 'focus groups say they [Films on Four] are a pleasure to watch because they have no special effects'.[50] He also stated that 'the industry is now schizoid . . . there is the Hollywood of the big action movies and big star names, but there are also the independents who make personal films based on character'.[51] By 1997, European cinema was also beginning to claw back box-office revenues for the first time in years. Whereas Hollywood films had once constituted 85–95% of the national box office in countries like the UK, Italy and Spain, on average that figure had dropped to 70%.[52] Furthermore, the success of small British films like *The Crying Game*, *Four Weddings and a Funeral*, *Trainspotting* and *The Full Monty* (Peter Cattaneo, 1997) in America had prompted Hollywood execs to take a closer look at European film, meaning that the industry was truly becoming more global, 'even as it begins to cater to more individual cultures'.[53] As one of the first major independent hits and European art-house/mainstream cross-over films, the success of *The Crying Game* played a part in facilitating greater production and distribution links between Europe and the USA, and also helped pave the way for the continued challenges of independent film to Hollywood's economic and cultural hegemony.

The growth of American independent companies has been crucial in the distribution and success of Films on Four in the USA. Miramax's distinctive marketing style led to the rise of the cross-over film, which has been fundamental in enabling small, low-budget British films to make an impact in the American market. *The Crying Game* represented Film on Four's first major global hit and was also an important benchmark in the growth of the American independent sector as the first indie film to take more than $60 million at the US box office. A study of the critical reception of *The Crying Game* has shown that, for American audiences, low-budget British films could provide a refreshing alternative to mainstream studio productions, and though the film's notorious and problematic marketing 'gimmick' was crucial to its widespread appeal, the popularity of the film was suggestive of a willingness to embrace more challenging, stylistically interesting productions. The popularity of *The Crying Game* in the USA has also shown that as well as being a crucial cornerstone for independent production and distribution in the UK and Europe, Channel 4-funded films have also been instrumental in the growth of the American independent sector in the 1980s and 1990s. The marketing techniques of US independents and their interest in British product was thus key to the success of Channel 4 films abroad, but also, as the following section will argue, to the channel's own approach to marketing films domestically.

Film Four International: Marketing *Trainspotting* and *East is East*

In the 1990s Channel 4 began to make its first forays into film and video distribution. In 1994, FFI started a video label with distributor First Independent, which was mainly intended for rental releases. First Independent already had a 'first look' deal with the channel whereby the company could opt to distribute Channel 4 films where FFI held the UK theatrical rights.[54] August 1995 saw the creation of Film Four Distributors. This was originally intended to be a joint venture with the Samuel Goldwyn Company but the deal fell apart due to financial difficulties. The company was headed by Nick Southworth and handled around twelve films per year, a mixture of third-party productions and those with Channel 4 backing.[55] In 1996, FFD also set up its own video rental arm under marketing head Colin Bunch.[56] These moves can be seen as direct precursors to the decision, in 1998, to incorporate the channel's film production, distribution and video interests into FilmFour, which would be run separately from the main channel under the leadership of Paul Webster.

Discourse in the British media around this time centred on the fact that British companies were making films like *The Full Monty* and *Trainspotting* that could be successful abroad but still retain distinctive elements intrinsic to British culture. Critics like Nick James began to argue that this increased American interest in British product led filmmakers to become deferential to American notions of 'Britishness'.[57] In conjunction with an increase in British production (unprecedented since the 1960s) due to tax breaks and the availability of lottery funding, there was a market for youthful, edgy British cinema. This was spurred on by an increased celebration of 'Brit' music and culture at this time. Unfortunately many of these films never saw the light of day due to the disparity between production and distribution in the UK: film production may have increased, but the problems endemic to the industry in terms of distributing and marketing feature films remained unchanged. Many of these films were criticised as shallow, vapid efforts which prioritised style over content in order to appeal to the all-important youth market. They seemed to typify everything that had come to be associated with the shallow and empty idea of 'Cool Britannia' – the celebration of British pop and fashion which was exploited by the Blair government in the late 1990s. *Shallow Grave, Trainspotting,* Guy Ritchie's *Lock, Stock and Two Smoking Barrels* (1998) and Shane Meadows's *24:7* (1998) gave rise to imitators such as *Shopping* (Paul W. S. Anderson, 1994), *Love, Honour and Obey* (Dominic Anciano and Ray Burdis, 2000) and *Gangster No. 1* (Paul McGuigan, 2000).[58] Meanwhile, companies like Miramax and PolyGram set about acquiring British product that embodied the magic formula of being just 'local' enough to give a distinctive flavour of British culture, but also 'universal' enough in theme to appeal to American audiences.

PolyGram's UK distribution of *Trainspotting* in 1996 drew on features popularised by American independents such as the 'platform' release and capitalising on word of mouth following showcases at key festivals. PFE and Rank (distributing in France, Belgium, Spain, Holland and Australia) bought the rights to the film and secured a February 1996 release date. PolyGram spent £850,000 on promoting the film, more money than was commonly invested in the marketing of British films domestically.[59] PFE marketing executive Julia Short told *Empire* that because the film was to be released in the UK first, the aim was to have an impact and to be seen as aggressive. PFE relied less on television and radio spots than on introducing the film's characters through posters on billboards around the country.[60] According to Chris Bailey, head of PFE's UK theatrical distribution, the campaign was to draw upon the success of *Shallow Grave* and be 'stylish and character-based', and indeed, the film's marketing campaign was to bear a strong resemblance to that for *Shallow Grave.*

A firm which specialised in designing record covers was hired to design the posters for *Trainspotting,* signifying the importance of the soundtrack to the film's popularity and PFE's desire to tap into the 'Brit-pop' audience.[61] The popular influence of the poster was profound, and its cultural cachet was used in everything from retail advertisements to political sketches. MGM Video even attempted to cash in on the cult value of the film to generate sales for its re-release of the British cult classic *Withnail & I* (Bruce Robinson, 1987). Like *Shallow Grave*, *Trainspotting* was shown out of competition at Cannes, as a means of showcasing the production to garner publicity. John Hodge, Andrew Macdonald and Danny Boyle gave numerous interviews together in the UK and abroad, following the film in its circuit around major territories. Once a small number of people had seen the film, word of mouth grew and was then fanned by strategic and controlled publicity.

FilmFour's UK marketing campaign for *East is East* followed a similar strategy. The film was originally developed by the BBC and commissioned by David Aukin for Film on Four, and was passed over to FilmFour when the company began in 1998. The new company consisted of FilmFour productions, FilmFour International, FilmFour Distribution and FilmFour Lab, and its remit was to operate more along the lines of a traditional film studio. As part of what Channel 4's new Chief Executive Michael Jackson called a 'kill the middle' strategy, FilmFour would support low-budget productions (under FilmFour Lab), larger-budget British and international productions, and Hollywood studio-type films. The structure of the new business enabled greater integration between production, marketing and distribution. Peter Buckingham, head of FilmFour distribution, said in 1999:

> What we have done over the past 12 months is to unify our campaigns a lot more between theatrical, video rental and then retail by literally bringing all the people involved into the same room and making sure they understood how we were marketing the films and making sure they had the information they need when they needed it.[62]

The company would also divert more energy into focusing on the European and North American markets. According to Paul Webster, the North American market was important to FilmFour, but having a film company associated with the European market was also a 'real strength'.[63] Webster, having previously worked for Palace's distribution arm as well as for Miramax, brought distribution into the heart of the decision-making process. One can note a strong American presence in FilmFour's slate for 1999/2000 and an increased interest in finding American co-production partners.

The UK release of *East is East* was, in some ways, an important landmark for the industry. For a market seen largely as a 'cottage' industry with a heavy reliance on companies like Rank for large-scale distribution, FilmFour was now operating almost as a mini-studio, overseeing everything from development to distribution. Producers, competitors and trade magazines kept a close eye on FilmFour's marketing strategies for the film. One distributor said that 'what FilmFour is doing is very interesting. If successful it will open the way for our films, for what would have been specialist releases, to get much greater exposure'. Teaser posters for the film were released in mid-October 1999, depicting a dog climbing on the *East is East* logo with a caption saying 'The Mutt's Nuts'. This was banned in Ireland because of its 'crudeness'.[64]

The main campaign was more conventional, depicting the cast with the tagline 'young, free, and soon not to be single'.[65] With earlier teaser posters designed to capture the younger audience, in this poster one can detect a certain universality of appeal – rather than being an Asian film about a Pakistani family struggling to reconcile traditional culture with British life, this tagline suggested a film about young people and the trials and tribulations of love – a theme to which many can relate. The more traditional ad would feature on 700 Adshell sites and 1,500 four-sheet posters, with ads also placed in newspapers from *The Sun* to *The Guardian*.[66] FilmFour decided to opt for the 'platform' approach when releasing the film, initially opening on seventy-two sites in the UK and Ireland, and then moving wider. At the same time, the FilmFour website featured a virtual dating game to tie in with these promotions.[67] Ads were also shown on television in between programmes like *The Big Breakfast*, *Frasier* and *Friends* to capture the 16–24 audience. The campaign cost $320,000 per week on average.[68] Instead of making a limited number of prints, 227 were made, unprecedented in the history of a Film on Four/FilmFour production.

The film received a standing ovation at Cannes, after which Miramax bought it for US release. However, the film did not do well in the USA, grossing just $4 million.[69] Like *Trainspotting*, for the American release of *East is East* some lines in the film were re-dubbed by the actors at the request of Miramax. However, Miramax attempted to play down any cultural elements of the film which might have been confusing to American audiences, whereas with *Trainspotting* it had capitalised on these features. The company had turned the perceived cultural disadvantages of *Trainspotting* into gimmicks to draw in audiences. One device was fanning speculation among audiences as to the cultural specificity of the film's title. In an article in *Empire*, David Elmer asked cinemagoers outside the premiere in LA what they thought the word 'Trainspotting' meant. Answers included:

> 'I think it means the tracks on someone's arms from heroin use.'
> 'I've heard that it's a game some people play in Scotland.'
> 'Does it have to do with cleaning up: you know, kicking the heroin?'
> 'Eh, the train is the rear end of a raptor, a birc of prey.'
> 'I was thinking more of a woman's ass.'[70]

In this way the difficult cultural translations of certain elements of the film became comic quirks rather than obstacles.[71]

Miramax was less confident in the handling of *East is East*. 'Our kid', a northern term referring to a family member, was replaced with the character's names, as the company thought Americans might mistake the term for a Pakistani name.[72] Certain British expressions were also changed – for example, 'what the 'eck' was changed to 'what the hell'.[73] Director Damien O'Donnell stated in an interview that he objected to changing the phrase 'the bin' to 'the trash' as he worried that the film was pandering too much to American audiences.[74] The bewildering nature of the poster used to promote the film may have been a factor in its failure to 'cross over'. The Miramax poster for *East is East* featured a blue-eyed blonde girl blowing bubblegum, wearing a tenement building as a hat. More White British than Asian British characters are depicted in the poster, despite the mainly Asian cast. O'Donnell, questioned about the racial element of the poster by the *Washington Post*, simply said 'I don't know what that's all about'.[75] Reactions to the film at the Washington International Film Festival were positive,[76] but *Associated Press* noted that its appeal in the UK didn't quite translate to American audiences:

> The script could have used another draft. The subplots aren't developed and the father's character especially feels underwritten, abruptly changing from amiable grouch to hateful tyrant. [Om] Puri, playing a confused, desperate man, did far better with a similar role in last year's *My Son the Fanatic*.[77]

It is difficult to isolate the elements of a film which enable it to gain popularity with international audiences. Paul Webster stated that

> *Lock, Stock* didn't work [in America] because in an invigorated marketplace the plethora of UK product means some films are only

> successful in the domestic market because of their specific, local
> appeal – whereas the *Full Monty*'s universality of story allowed it
> to cross over. We think that our upcoming film, *East is East*, has the
> ability to do that.[78]

However, with *East is East*, American critics and audiences did not have as much to relate to as they did with *Trainspotting*. Though more firmly entrenched in its specific, regional culture than *East is East*, the soundtrack and 'Brit-pop' element of *Trainspotting* was integral to its success.[79] Through the film's link with music and its vibrant, youthful feel, American critics could draw references between *Trainspotting* and popular British films like Richard Lester's *A Hard Day's Night* (1964). In its stylistic elements and depiction of violence, it could be compared to films by Tarantino and the Coen brothers, while also harking back to films like *A Clockwork Orange* (Stanley Kubrick, 1971). As we have seen, then, the cross-cultural appeal of a film can depend upon a combination of shrewd marketing strategies, the types of films available to audiences at the time of release, universality of story/theme and the film's relationship with the popular culture of that era.

East is East was received very well in the UK, although some criticisms of the film indicate that FilmFour was still struggling to shake off its links to television broadcasting. The *Turriff Advertiser* said that the film was 'more telly/video fare than big screen, but there are fine performances from all the cast, a fair sparkling of humorous one liners . . .'[80] while *The Sun* noted that it was 'the sort of British film that is destined to turn up on Channel 4 telly after doing award winning business at some snooty film festivals'.[81] *Trainspotting*, on the other hand, was seldom confused with television, perhaps due to the more surreal and stylistic elements of the film, as well as the global popularity of the soundtrack.

The success of *East is East* led to an increase in media discourse around the Asian experience in Britain, with attention drawn to Asian theatre productions (*East is East* started life as a play), the contentious issue of arranged marriages among young Asian Britons, and the growing number of Asian people moving into television and film. References were drawn to films like Gurinder Chadha's *Bhaji on the Beach* (1993) and programmes like *Goodness Gracious Me* (1998–2001). At the same time, it was noted that *East is East* also drew heavily on the British New Wave aesthetic, with the *Evening Standard* stating that the film, with its depiction of northern working-class British realism and humour, was rooted firmly in the 'comedy of the kitchen sink'.[82] In Britain, its marketing campaign aimed at wider universal appeal, while still firmly rooted in British cinematic traditions of social realism and working-class comedy. Despite being commissioned by Film on Four under David Aukin, *East is East* came to be seen as one of the few major successes of FilmFour before it was subsumed by Channel 4 in 2002.

Conclusion

International breakout hits like *The Crying Game* and *Four Weddings and a Funeral*, *Trainspotting* and *East is East* had shown that British films could actually make money in the domestic market. A comparison of these films shows how the market for British films had changed, both at home and abroad. *East is East*, in particular, shows how Channel 4's longstanding relationship with PolyGram and Miramax influenced the marketing techniques of FilmFour as a standalone company. An analysis of how *Trainspotting* and *East is East* fared in the American market can also give us an insight into how American critics and audiences responded to these films, and the marketing and promotional campaigns surrounding them. Channel 4 films have impacted other national cinemas and influenced the reputation of British film abroad, which in turn has also influenced perceptions of Channel 4 films in the UK. As the case study of *The Crying Game* illustrates, a film which barely broke even in the British market could become a global hit, garnering positive reviews and Oscar nominations. A key theme to emerge from these two case studies is the extent to which Films on Four continued to be closely associated with television for UK critics. As the studies of critical reception in this chapter have illustrated, Films on Four tended to be branded as small-scale productions associated with television, aesthetically and financially. However, this chapter has shown that these films could have different connotations for other national audiences, which was in large part determined by their marketing.

Finally, this chapter has looked at Channel 4's own film distribution practices in the late 1990s. The marketing behind *Trainspotting* shows the influence of the strategies of American independents on the distribution of Films on Four in the UK in the 1990s, while *East is East* illustrates that, while FilmFour was utilising these strategies to distribute a low-budget film on a large scale for the first time, Miramax, at the same time, could also get it badly wrong. In comparison to the slate of productions commissioned by FilmFour in 1998/1999, *East is East* was undoubtedly a commission left over from Film on Four under Aukin. A film about the struggles of a British Pakistani family living in a working-class area in the 1970s presented a stark contrast to the higher-budget productions that FilmFour was becoming involved in at this time. Under Paul Webster Channel 4's strategies changed radically as it attempted to navigate a more competitive environment under a more commercial remit.

Notes

1. Peter Biskind, *Down and Dirty Pictures: Miramax, Sundance and the Rise of Independent Film* (London: Bloomsbury, 2004), 18.
2. Martin Dale, *The Movie Game: Film Business in Britain, Europe and America* (New York: Continuum International Publishing Group Ltd, 1997), 58.
3. *Ibid.*
4. *Ibid.*
5. *Ibid.*, 75.
6. Thomas Elsaesser, *European Cinema: Face to Face with Hollywood* (Amsterdam: Amsterdam University Press, 2005), 46.
7. Any study of Miramax must be viewed in the context of the allegations which emerged in 2017 regarding the long history of abuse perpetuated by the convicted rapist, sex offender and co-founder of the company, Harvey Weinstein. Under consideration here is Miramax's influence in partially defining the marketing and distribution template followed by much of the American independent sector in the early 1990s. The company name 'Miramax' will be used throughout this section, with no references made to Weinstein as the company's co-founder.
8. Biskind, *Down and Dirty Pictures*, 55.
9. John Berra, *Declarations of Independence: American Cinema and the Partiality of Independent Production* (Chicago: Intellect, 2008), 161.
10. Biskind, *Down and Dirty Pictures*, 55.
11. Pierre Bourdieu, *The Field of Cultural Production* (Oxford: Polity Press, 1993), 77.
12. Dale, *The Movie Game*, 62.
13. Geoff King, *Indiewood, USA: Where Hollywood Meets Independent Cinema* (New York: I. B. Tauris, 2009), 93.
14. Berra, *Declarations of Independence*, 161.
15. *Ibid.*, 171.
16. Dale, *The Movie Game*, 62.
17. King, *Indiewood, USA*, 2–4.
18. Berra, *Declarations of Independence*, 161.
19. Angus Finney, *The Egos Have Landed: The Rise and Fall of Palace Pictures* (London: William Heinemann, 1996), 143–4.
20. Kate Robinson, personal communication, 18 September 2012.
21. Anon., 'Interview with Stephen Woolley', *Premiere* (April 1993), 77.
22. *Time Magazine*, 20 March 1993.

23. *LA Times*, 23 February 1993.
24. King, *Indiewood, USA*, 7.
25. *LA Times*, 23 February 1993.
26. Anon., 'Interview with Stephen Woolley', *Premiere* (April 1993), 77.
27. *Financial Times*, 29 October 1992.
28. *The Guardian*, 22 October 1992.
29. *Times Magazine*, 5 June 1993.
30. Anon., 'Interview with Stephen Woolley', 77.
31. *The Guardian*, 20 February 1993.
32. *Ibid.*
33. The *New Yorker*, 16 November 1992.
34. *LA Daily News*, 25 November 1992.
35. The *New Yorker*, 16 November 1992.
36. *New York Times*, 5 January 1993.
37. *The Orange County Register*, 24 November 1992.
38. *Entertainment Weekly*, 12 February 1998.
39. *Sunday Times*, 28 March 1993.
40. *Sunday Times*, 21 February 1993.
41. Berra, *Declarations of Independence*, 138.
42. *The Guardian* 12 August 1993
43. *Premiere*, January 1994.
44. Andrew Higson, 'The Limiting Imagination of National Cinema', in *Transnational Cinema, the Film Reader*, ed. by Elizabeth Ezra and Terry Rowden (London: Routledge, 2006), 16–20.
45. Nick James, 'They Think It's All Over: British Cinema's US Surrender', in *The British Cinema Book*, ed. by Robert Murphy, 2nd edn (London: BFI Publishing, 2002), 303.
46. *Sunday Times*, 1 November 1994.
47. *Daily Telegraph*, 29 October 1994.
48. *The Independent*, 29 October 1994.
49. *Financial Times*, 1 November 1994.
50. *The Observer*, 23 March 1997.
51. *Ibid.*
52. *Christian Science Monitor*, 18 March 1998.
53. *Ibid.*
54. *Screen Finance*, 26 January 1994, 3.
55. *Screen Finance*, 12 July 1995, 12.
56. *Screen Finance*, 1 May 1997, 18.
57. James, 'They Think It's All Over', 303.
58. *Ibid.*
59. *Screen International*, 9 February 1996.
60. *Empire*, 90 (March 1996), 90–102
61. *Screen International*, 9 February 1996.
62. *Video Home Entertainment*, 7 August 1999, 13.
63. *Hollywood Reporter*, 21 September 1999, 16.
64. *Screen International*, 5 November 1999.

65. *Ibid.*
66. *Ibid.*
67. *Ibid.*
68. *Ibid.*
69. *Variety*, 8–14 January 2001.
70. *Empire*, 98 (October 1996), 16.
71. *Ibid.*
72. *The Washington Post*, 16 April 2000.
73. *Ibid.*
74. *Ibid.*
75. *Ibid.*
76. *Ibid.*
77. *The Associated Press*, 10 April 2000.
78. *The Hollywood Reporter*, 21 September 1999.
79. Sarah Street, *Transatlantic Crossings: British Feature Films in the USA* (London: Continuum, 2002), 207.
80. *The Turriff Advertiser*, 3 December 1999.
81. *The Sun*, 6 November 1999.
82. *Evening Standard*, 4 November 1999.

Conclusion: Archives and the broadcaster's memory

In the summer of 2021, the UK's Conservative government opened a ministerial document for public consultation on whether Channel 4 should move from public to private ownership. This document argued for the immense importance of Channel 4's public service remit, before making the case that while the channel's remit has historically been of great value to British broadcasting, it is also becoming increasingly restrictive, with the result that the channel is no longer able to respond to the demands of the current competitive market. The document argues that the old model of broadcasting, which left Channel 4 reliant on advertising revenue from linear broadcasting, is unsuited to an era in which VoD providers need no public service remit and can borrow substantial amounts of money to fund high-quality programming aimed at audiences who prefer a non-linear model. The document retrospectively placed the idea of 'consumer choice' and revenue at the forefront of its framing of Public Service Broadcasting (PSB) and broadcasting history. While the Conservative government did create Channel 4, that decision had been decades in the making, and while 'consumer choice' was undoubtedly at stake, this framing is biased and lacking in context. One of the main issues that led to the creation of Channel 4 was that the broadcasters did not effectively cater to the experiences of black, Asian and ethnic-minority Britons, disabled people, the LGBT+ community, the young, the working class and those living outside of metropolitan areas. More choice, in terms of number of channels, has simply failed to address these issues, because it does not follow that greater choice must necessarily lead to greater representation. But the document was accurate in at least one respect: VoD providers and commercial streaming services have no need to meet a PSB remit, and they do not have to observe the policies of regulators in the same way as British broadcasters do. But this, surely, is the strength of Public Service Broadcasting – it is not choice but content that matters. It is not the largest number of people served, but that different communities are heard. Public Service Broadcasting is, to paraphrase the wording of early Channel 4 promotional material, 'for all of the people, some of the time'. The document also mentioned Channel 4's contribution to the British film industry: 'Channel 4 began broadcasting in November 1982, and the arrival of Richard Attenborough as Chairman in 1987 signalled the start of Channel 4's long involvement with the UK film industry too.' This statement's factual inaccuracy – by 1987, Film on Four had funded dozens of productions, and though cinema exhibition was still being negotiated by the mid-to-late 1980s, 1987 was also the year that Head of Drama David Rose received the Rossellini Award for 'Services to Cinema' at Cannes – shows that it is not just broadcasters who are prone to forgetting their own history.

In considering how the channel considers how its own role as a film financier has developed from 1982 to the present day, two points stand out as being particularly significant. Firstly, how the Channel views its own impact on British cinema depends to a large extent on the channel's position in the marketplace and on how it seeks to construct its own brand identity. As well as a production outfit, Film4 is also brand, and this brand identity is strongly linked to the channel's reputation as 'editor of choice', attracting consumers and in effect shaping consumer taste. How the channel views its own contribution to film culture is inextricably tied up with this role. Secondly, it is important to remember that for Channel 4, commerce and creativity, commercial considerations and cultural achievement are today too closely aligned to be considered as separate, never mind opposing, forces. That does not mean that Film4 aspires to be a Hollywood studio, nor does it mean that taking risks, supporting innovation, and cultural significance are any less important. In the 1980s, the relationship between commerce and culture was perhaps more polarised, but much has changed in response to a more fragmented marketplace, digital television, new viewing platforms and Video on Demand.

In a sense, focusing on the present is understandable: when struggling to remain afloat in a digital landscape that is changing rapidly, what on earth is the value of looking to the past? It is important that Channel 4 be agile and able to respond to a changing marketplace, but it is also the case that historical work can deepen our understanding of the real value and importance of a model of broadcasting that places viewers and services at the heart of its policies and strategies. What was also missing from the conversation around Channel 4's moves towards privatisation was the importance of PSB broadcasters to communities, regions and citizens. Netflix cannot provide local news to people in Yorkshire, and while VoD platforms might be good at funding new talent and even allowing a certain latitude in terms of creativity, they have different motivations to consider when deciding whether to commission a sitcom set in Hull.

History shows us that Channel 4 has been at its most successful when it has allowed programme makers the capacity to innovate. The most interesting creative decisions have been taken on little money and with the understanding that economic motivations are secondary to cultural ones. The films which are prized and remembered culturally are those specific to a time and place, not those which are made with a view to box-office success and specifically aimed at an international market. Film4 has been so successful because it has benefitted from two things that film studios, big or small, do not typically have: a public service remit and institutional acceptance (even expectation) of a business model that is financially unsustainable. Channel 4 has been synonymous with the most critically rated and interesting examples of British film culture for almost forty years precisely because making money from film (with the exception of the failed 1998–2002 FilmFour studio venture) has rarely been the channel's overriding aim. One of the most important things that broadcast history can teach us is this: for culture to be truly interesting, it must be afforded the space to fail.

Appendix: Channel 4 Features 1982–1998

Title	Year	Country	Production company	TX
Walter	1982	GB	Central Television	02/11/1982
Ptang Yang Kipperbang	1982	GB	Goldcrest Films and Television, Channel Four, Enigma Television	03/11/1982
Remembrance	1982	GB	Colin Gregg Films, Channel Four	10/11/1982
Praying Mantis	1982	GB	Portman Productions, Channel Four	17/11/1982
Praying Mantis pt 2	1982	GB	Portman Productions, Channel Four	24/11/1982
Giro City	1982	GB	Silvarealm, Channel Four, Rediffusion Films	01/12/1982
The Disappearance of Harry	1982	GB	Labrahurst Films, Channel Four	08/12/1982
Bad Hats	1982	GB	Les Productions Audiovisuelles, Skreba Films, TF1 Films Production	15/12/1982
Hero	1982	Scotland	Maya Films (Scotland), Channel Four	29/12/1982
Runners	1983	GB	Hanstoll Enterprises, Goldcrest Films and Television	17/05/1983
Angel	1982	Ireland, GB	Bord Scannán na hÉireann, Channel Four Films, Motion Picture Company of Ireland	28/04/1983
Moonlighting	1982	GB	Channel Four	05/05/1983
The Draughtsman's Contract	1982	GB	British Film Institute, Channel Four Television Company	30/06/1983
Ill Fares the Land	1983	GB	Scottish and Global Tv, Portman Productions	19/05/1983

Walter and June	1983	GB	Central Independent Television	26/05/1983
Living Apart Together	1983	Scotland	Legion Films, Darkbeem	02/06/1983
Nelly's Version	1983	GB	Mithras Films	09/06/1983
Red Monarch	1983	GB	Goldcrest Films and Television, Enigma Productions	16/06/1983
The Bad Sister	1983	GB	The Moving Picture Company, Modelmark	23/06/1983
The Ploughman's Lunch	1983	GB	Greenpoint Films, A.C. & D. (Plant Hirers), Goldcrest Films and Television, Michael White	03/11/1983
Another Time, Another Place	1983	GB	Rediffusion Films, Umbrella Films, Channel Four, Scottish Arts Council	10/11/1983
Those Glory Glory Days	1983	GB	Enigma Films Ltd, Goldcrest Films and Television, Channel Four	17/11/1983
The Country Girls	1983	GB	London Films International, Channel Four, Bord Scannán na hÉireann	24/11/1983
Meantime	1983	GB	Central Productions, Mostpoint, Channel Four	01/12/1983
Good and Bad at Games	1983	GB	Portman Productions, Quintet Films	08/12/1983
A Flame to the Phoenix	1983	GB	Granada Television	15/12/1983
Accounts	1983	GB	Partners in Production	22/12/1983
First Love: Sharma and Beyond	1984	GB	Enigma/Goldcrest	24/05/1984
Squaring the Circle	1984	GB	TVS in assoc. with Metromedia and Britannic Film and TV	31/05/1984
The Last Day of Summer	1983	GB	The Moving Picture Company	07/06/1984
The Outcasts	1982	GB	Tolymax	14/06/1984
Flight to Berlin	1983	German Federal Republic, GB	Road Movies Filmproduktion GmbH, British Film Institute Production Board, Channel Four	21/06/1984
In the White City/ Dans La Ville Blanche	1983	Portugal, Switzerland, GB	Metro Filme, Filmograph, WDR – Westdeutscher Rundfunk, Channel Four, SSR Télévision Suisse	28/06/1984
Reflections	1983	GB	Court House Films, Channel Four	05/07/1984
Loose Connections	1984	GB	Umbrella/Greenpoint	09/05/1985
Sacred Hearts	1984	GB	Stern TV for Channel 4 and ZDF	16/05/1985
A Song for Europe	1985	GB, German Federal Republic	ZDF – Zweites Deutsches Fernsehen, Stern TV, Gruner & Jahr, Channel Four	23/05/1985

Summer Lightning	1985	Ireland, Great Britain	Radio-Telefís Éireann, Film Four International, Channel Four	30/05/1985
Forever Young	1985	GB	Enigma Television, Goldcrest Films and Television	06/06/1985
El Norte	1983	USA, GB	Inc. Independent Productions, American Playhouse	13/06/1985
Singleton's Pluck, alt title Laughterhouse	1984	GB	Ltd. Laughterhouse, Greenpoint Films, Film Four International	12/12/1985
Christmas Present	1985	GB	Telekation International	19/12/1985
The Eyes of Birds	1982	France, GB	Forum Films, Plaisance Productions Télévision Suisse Romande, Antenne 2, Channel Four	13/03/1986
Strawberry Fields	1985	German Federal Republic, GB	Marten Täge Filmproducktion, Channel Four	20/03/1986
The King and the Queen	1985	Spain, GB	TVE Televisión Española, Channel Four, SACIS, RAI	27/03/1986
Heat and Dust	1983	GB	Merchant Ivory	22/05/1986
Paris Texas	1984	German Federal Republic, France, GB	Road Movies Filmproduktion GmbH, Argos-Films, WDR – Westdeutscher Rundfunk, Channel Four, Project Filmproduktion im Filmverlag der Autoren	29/05/1986
Letters to an Unknown Lover	1985	GB, France	Portman Productions, Antenne 2, Channel Four	05/06/1986
Wetherby	1985	GB	Greenpoint Films	12/06/1986
The Innocent	1984	GB	Tempest Films, Television South	19/06/1986
Success is the Best Revenge	1984	GB, France	De Vere Studio, Société Nouvelle des Etablissements Gaumont, Emerald Film Partnership, Ministère Français de la Culture	26/06/1986
The Chain	1984	GB	Quintet Films & Television, County Bank, Film Four International	12/02/1987
My Beautiful Laundrette	1987	GB	Channel Four, Working Title Films, SAF Productions	19/02/1987
Cal	1984	GB	Ltd. Eastern Counties Newspapers Group, Enigma Productions, Warner Bros, Goldcrest Films and Television, United Film Distribution Company	26/02/1987
The Company of Wolves	1984	GB	Palace Productions	05/03/1987
She'll Be Wearing Pink Pyjamas	1984	GB	Pink Pyjama Productions, Film Four International	12/03/1987
No Surrender	1985	GB, Canada	No Surrender Films, Dumbarton Films, National Film Finance Corporation, Film Four International, Lauron International	19/03/1987

Another Country	1984	GB	Goldcrest	26/03/1987
Billy the Kid and the Green Baize Vampire	1985	GB	ITC Entertainment, Zenith Productions	02/04/1987
Insignificance	1985	GB	Zenith in assoc with The Recorded Picture Company	09/04/1987
The Assam Garden	1984	GB	The Moving Picture Company	16/04/1987
Restless Natives	1985	GB	Oxford Film Company	23/04/1987
A Zed and Two Noughts	1985	GB	British Film Institute Production Board, Artificial Eye Productions, Film Four International, Allarts Enterprises	30/04/1987
Letter to Brezhnev	1985	GB	Yeardream, Film Four International, Palace Productions	07/05/1987
Caravaggio	1986	GB	British Film Institute, Channel Four Television	14/05/1987
Vagabonde	1985	France, GB	Ciné-Tamaris, Films A2	04/06/1987
Voyage to Cythera	1984	Greece, German Federal Republic	Theo Angelopoulos Film Productions, Elliniko Kentro Kinimatographou, ZDF – Zweites Deutsches Fernsehen, RAI, ET, Channel Four	18/06/1987
Dance with a Stanger	1985	GB	First Film Company, Goldcrest Films and Television, National Film Finance Corporation, Film Four International	03/03/1988
Heavenly Pursuits	1986	GB	Island Films, Skreba Films, Film Four International, National Film Finance Corporation	17/03/1988
Lamb	1985	GB	Flickers Productions, Limehouse Productions, Channel Four	24/03/1988
Maschenka	1988	German Federal Republic, GB, France, Finland	Clasart Filmund Fernsehproduktion, Jörn Donner Productions, Suomen Elokuvasäätiö, ZDF, Channel Four, France 3	31/03/1988
Eat the Peach	1986	Ireland	Strongbow Productions, Film Four International	07/04/1988
Born of Fire	1986	GB	Dehlavi Films	14/04/1988
Shadey	1985	GB	Film Four International, Larkspur Films	28/04/1988
The Good Father	1988	GB	Greenpoint	12/05/1988
The Belly of an Architect	1987	GB, Italy	Mondial, Tangram Film, The Callender Company, Hemdale Holdings, SACIS, Gavin Film	16/02/1989
The Sacrifice	1986	Sweden, France, GB	Svenska Filminstitutet, Argos-Films, Film Four International, Josephson & Nykvist, Sveriges Television TV2, Sandrew Film & Teater, Ministère Français de la Culture	18/02/1989

Mona Lisa	1986	GB	HandMade Films, Palace Pictures	23/02/1989
High Season	1987	GB	Hemdale Film Corporation, Marlie Productions Ltd, Forever Films, Curzon Film Distributors, Channel Four, National Film Development Fund, British Screen Finance	02/03/1989
Hidden City	1987	GB	Hidden City Films, Film Four International, ZDF – Zweites Deutsches Fernsehen	09/03/1989
Genesis	1986	France, India, Belgium, Switzerland	Scarabée Films, Mrinal Sen Productions, Les Films de la Drève, Cactus Film, Film Four International, SSR Télévision Suisse	16/03/1989
Prick Up Your Ears	1987	GB	Zenith Productions, Civilhand, British Screen, Channel Four	16/03/1989
Ping Pong	1986	GB	Picture Palace Productions, Film Four International	23/03/1989
The Nature of the Beast	1988	GB	Rosso Productions, Film Four International, British Screen	30/03/1989
Good Morning Babylon	1987	Italy, France, USA	Filmtre, MK2 Productions, Edward R. Pressman Film Corporation, RAI, Films A2, Cinecittà [1985]	06/04/1989
Yerma	1985	German Federal Republic, Hungary, Canada	Magyar Televízió, Starfilm, Starfilm Martin Moszkowicz, Makropus-Film, Hunnia Játekfilmstudió, Sefel Pictures, Channel Four	08/04/1989
A Room With a View	1985	GB	Merchant Ivory Productions Ltd	13/04/1989
The Road Home	1987	Poland, GB	Zed Productions, Zespol Filmowy 'Tor'	15/04/1989
Fatherland	1986	GB, German Federal Republic, France	Film Four International, Clasart Film- und Fernsehproduktion, MK2 Productions, Kestrel II, Ministère Français de la Culture	20/04/1989
Comrades	1987	GB	National Film Trustee Company Ltd, Skreba Films, National Film Finance Corporation, Film Four International, Curzon Film Distributors, David Hannay Productions	27/04/1989
Playing Away	1986	GB	Film Four International, Insight Productions, Channel Four	04/05/1989
Leave to Remain	1988	GB	Spellbound Productions	11/05/1989
Milk and Honey	1988	Canada, GB	J.A. Film Company, Zenith Productions, Téléfilm Canada, Ontario Media Development Corporation, First Choice Canadian Communications Corporation, Sundance Institute	18/05/1989

No Man's Land	1985	Switzerland, France, German Federal Republic, GB	Filmograph, MK2 Productions, SSR Télévision Suisse, WDR – Westdeutscher Rundfunk, Films A2, Channel Four	15/02/1990
Wish You Were Here	1987	GB	Zenith Productions, Working Title Films, Film Four International	15/02/1990
The Dead	1987	GB, USA, German Federal Republic	Zenith Productions, Liffey Films, Vestron Pictures, Channel Four, Delta Film	22/02/1990
High Hopes	1988	GB	Portman Productions, British Screen, Channel Four	01/03/1990
The Mirror	1984	German Federal Republic	Von Vietinghof Filmproduktion, ZDF – Zweites Deutsches Fernsehen, Channel Four	08/03/1990
Sammy and Rosie Get Laid	1987	GB	Sammy and Rosie Limited, Working Title Films, Cinecom Entertainment Group, British Screen Finance Channel Four	08/03/1990
Vertiges	1985	France	Les Films du Passage	15/03/1990
Wild Flowers	1990	GB	Channel Four Television Company, Frontroom Productions, Channel Four	15/03/1990
Vroom	1988	GB	Motion Pictures Productions, Film Four International, British Screen	22/03/1990
The Kitchen Toto	1987	GB	Skreba Films, Cannon Films (UK), B.V. Cannon International, British Screen, Film Four International	29/03/1990
Maurice	1987	GB	Merchant Ivory Productions Ltd	05/04/1990
The Final Frame	1989	GB	Kinesis Films	12/04/1990
A Month in the Country	1987	GB	Euston Films, Channel Four, Pennies from Heaven	19/04/1990
Conquest of the South Pole	1990	Scotland	Jam Jar Films, Channel Four	26/04/1990
Landscape in the Mist	1988	Greece, France, Italy	Elliniko Kentro Kinimatographou, ET-1, Paradis Films, Basic Cinematografica	28/04/1990
On the Black Hill	1987	GB	British Film Institute, British Screen	03/05/1990
Rita, Sue and Bob, Too	1987	GB	British Screen, Umbrella Entertainment	10/05/1990
Hotel du Paradis	1986	France, GB	Umbrella-Portman Productions	24/05/1990
In Fading Light	1989	GB	Amber Films	31/05/1990
A World Apart	1988	GB, Zimbabwe	Working Title	21/04/1991
Hope and Glory	1987	GB	Goldcrest, Nelson Entertainment	28/04/1991
Drowning by Numbers	1988	GB, Netherlands	Allarts Enterprises/ VPRO/ Nederlandse Omroep Stichting/ Elsevier-Vendex Film Beheer/ Channel Four	05/05/1991

We Think the World of You	1988	GB, USA	Cinecom Pictures	12/05/1991
Smack and Thistle	1989	GB	Working Title, Channel 4	19/05/1991
The Dressmaker	1987	GB	Dressmaker Productions, Channel Four, British Screen	26/05/1991
Life Is Sweet	1991	GB	Thin Man Films	15/09/1992
Riff-Raff	1991	GB	Parallax Pictures	22/09/1992
Paris by Night	1988	GB	British Screen, Film Four International, Zenith Productions, Greenpoint Films, Cineplex Odeon Films	29/09/1992
Venus, Peter	1989	GB	BFI, Channel Four, Scottish Film Production Fund, Orkney Islands Council, British Screen	06/10/1992
Queen of Hearts	1989	GB, USA	Enterprise Pictures TVS Films Ltd, Nelson Entertainment, Film Four International, Telso International	13/10/1992
December Bride	1990	Ireland, GB	Little Bird Company Limited, Film Four International, Central Independent Television, British Screen, Ulster TV, Radio-Telefís Éireann	20/10/1992
Diamond Skulls	1989	GB	Working Title, British Screen	24/10/1992
Stormy Monday	1988	GB, USA	National Film Trustee Company Ltd, The Moving Picture Company, British Screen, Film Four International, Atlantic Entertainment Group	27/10/1992
Bye Bye Baby	1992	GB	Paravision	03/11/1992
Resurrected	1989	GB	St Pancras Films, Film Four International, British Screen	10/11/1992
I Hired a Contract Killer	1990	Finland, Sweden, France, GB, German Federal Republic	Villealfa Filmproductions Oy, Svenska Filminstitutet, Finnkino, Megamania, Esselte Video, Pyramide Productions, Channel Four, Pandora Filmproduktion, Suomen Elokuvasäätiö, First City Features	17/11/1992
The Deceivers	1988	GB	Merchant Ivory Productions Ltd, Michael White, Cinecom Entertainment Group, Film Four International	01/12/1992
Sour Sweet	1987	GB	National Film Trustee Company Ltd, First Film Company, British Screen, Zenith Productions, Film Four International, Curzon Film Distributors, National Film Development Fund, Park Street Film Developments	08/12/1992

Strapless	1988	GB	Granada Film Productions	15/12/1992
Fools of Fortune	1989	Ireland	PolyGram Filmproduktion GmbH, Palace Pictures, PolyGram, Working Title Films	22/12/1992
The Fool	1990	GB	Sands Films	25/12/1992
God on the Rocks	1990	GB	Skreba Films	29/12/1992
Hear My Song	1991	GB	Film Four International, Vision Productions, Limelight Films, British Screen, Windmill Lane Productions	21/10/1993
Close My Eyes	1991	GB	Beambright Productions	29/10/1993
Paper Mask	1990	GB	Film Four international, Granada and British Screen	04/11/1993
Young Soul Rebels	1991	GB, Germany, France, Spain	Film Four International, Sankofa Film & Video, La Sept Kinowelt and Iberoamericana	11/11/1993
The Miracle	1990	GB, Ireland	Palace Productions, Promenade Productions, British Screen	19/11/1993
Blonde Fist	1990	GB, USA	Film Four International, Glinwood Films, Blonde Fist Ltd	25/11/1993
Closing Numbers	1993	GB	Arden Films	02/12/1993
Trust	1990	GB, USA	Zenith in association with True Fiction Pictures	09/12/1993
The Bridge	1991	GB	Moonlight Films	16/12/1993
Shuttlecock	1991	GB, France.	KM Films, Les Productions Belles Rives	06/01/1994
One Man's War	1990	GB, USA.	Television South, Skreba Films, HBO Showcase, Film Four International	20/01/1994
Prospero's Books	1991	Netherlands, France, Italy, Great Britain, Japan	Allarts Enterprses, Cinéa, Caméra One, Penta Pictures, Elsevier-Vendex Film Beheer, Film Four International, VPRO, Canal+, Nippon Hoso Kyokai, Eurimages Conseil de l'Europe, Stichting Produktiefonds voor Nederlandse Films, Heldring & Pierson Pierson	27/01/1994
The Crying Game	1992	GB	Channel Four, Palace (Soldier's Wife) Ltd, Nippon Film Development & Finance, Palace Productions, Eurotrustees, British Screen	01/11/1994
Peter's Friends	1992	GB, USA	Renaissance Films, The Samuel Goldwyn Company, Channel 4 Films	08/11/1994
Waterland	1992	GB, USA	Palace Pictures Pandora Cinema, Channel Four, British Screen	15/11/1994
Wild West	1992	GB	Channel Four Television Company, Initial Film and Television, Wild West	22/11/1994

Bad Behaviour	1993	GB	Film Four International, Parallax Pictures, Channel Four, British Screen, First Independent Films Ltd	29/11/1994
London Kills Me	1991	GB	PolyGram Filmed Entertainment, London Kills Me Limited, Working Title Films, Channel Four	06/12/1994
Secret Friends	1991	GB	Whistling Gypsy Production, Film Four International	13/12/1994
Into the West	1992	Ireland, GB, USA	Talbot Film Distributors, Little Bird Company Limited, Parallel Film Productions, Majestic Films International, Miramax Film Corporation, Channel Four, British Screen, Newcomm	21/12/1994
Simple Men	1992	GB, USA, Italy	Zenith Productions, American Playhouse Theatrical Films, True Fiction Pictures, Fine Line Productions, Film Four International, BIM Distribuzione, Public Broadcasting Service, Corporation for Public Broadcasting, National Endowment for the Arts, Chubb Group of Insurance Companies	03/01/1995
The Long Day Closes	1992	GB	Film Four International, British Film Institute Production	10/01/1995
Dust Devil	1992	GB, USA	Palace (Devil) Ltd, Palace Productions, Film Four International, British Screen, Miramax Films	16/05/1995
Willie's War	1994	GB	Children's Film Unit	09/07/1995
Howards End	1992	GB, Japan	Merchant Ivory Productions Ltd, Film Four International, Sumitomo Group, Imagica, Cinema Ten Corporation, Japan Satellite Broadcasting, IDE Productions	10/10/1995
This Boy's Story	1992	GB	National Film and Television School, Channel Four	17/10/1995
Damage	1992	GB, France	Skreba Films, Nouvelles Éditions de Films, European Co-Production Fund (UK), Channel Four, Le Studio Canal+, Majestic Films International	24/10/1995
Raining Stones	1993	GB	Channel Four Television Corporation, Parallax Pictures, Channel Four, Film Four International	31/10/1995
The Ballad of the Sad Café	1991	GB	Merchant Ivory Productions Ltd	07/11/1995

Four Weddings and a Funeral	1993	GB	PolyGram Filmproduktion GmbH, Working Title Films, PolyGram Filmed Entertainment, Channel 4 Films	15/11/1995
Naked	1993	GB	Thin Man Films	21/11/1995
Friends	1994	GB, France	Friends Productions, Chrysalide Films, Rio, Channel 4 Films, British Screen, Canal+, European Co-Production Fund (UK)	28/11/1995
Oleanna	1994	USA	Goldwyn Entertainment Company, Channel 4 Films, Bay Kinescope	05/12/1995
My Crazy Life (Mi Vida Loca)	1993	GB, USA	Inc. Cineville Partners III, CineVille, HBO Showcase, Film Four International, Sundance Institute, Inc. Cineville Partners III	12/12/1995
No Worries	1993	Australia, GB	Palm Beach Pictures, Initial Films	26/12/1995
A Pin for the Butterfly	1994	GB, Czech Republic	Skreba Films, Heureka Production	16/01/1996
Three Colours: Blue	1993	France, Switzerland, Poland	MK2 Productions, CEO Productions, France 3 Cinéma, CAB Productions, Zespol Filmowy 'Tor', Canal+, Eurimages Conseil de l'Europe, CNC – Centre national de la cinématographie	06/07/1996
Three Colours White	1993	France, Switzerland, Poland	MK2 Productions, France 3 Cinéma, CAB Productions, Zespol Filmowy 'Tor', Canal+, Eurimages Conseil de l'Europe	13/07/1996
Three Colours Red	1994	France, Switzerland, Poland	MK2 Productions, France 3 Cinéma, CAB Productions, Zespol Filmowy 'Tor', Canal+, Eurimages Conseil de l'Europe, Télévision Suisse Romande, L'Office Fédéral de la Culture Suisse du Département	20/07/1996
In Custody	1993	GB	Merchant Ivory	11/11/1996
The Madness of King George	1994	GB, USA	Mad George Films Ltd, The Samuel Goldwyn Company, Close Call Films, Channel 4 Films	25/11/1996
Ladybird, Ladybird	1994	GB	Channel Four Television Corporation, Parallax Pictures, Film Four International	28/11/1996
Backbeat	1993	United Germany, GB	PolyGram Filmproduktion GmbH, PolyGram Filmed Entertainment, Scala Productions, Channel 4 Films, Scala/Woolley/Powell/Dyer, Forthcoming Productions	05/12/1996
Bhaji on the Beach	1994	GB	Channel Four Television Corporation, Umbi Films, Channel Four, Film Four International	12/12/1996

Shopping	1993	GB, USA	Channel Four Television Corporation, Impact Pictures, Channel Four, PolyGram Filmed Entertainment, Kuzui Enterprises, WMG Pictures	19/12/1996
Vanya on 42nd Street	1994	USA, GB	Vanya Company Inc, Mayfair Entertainment International, Channel 4 Films, Laura Pels Productions, New Media Finance	26/12/1996
Death and the Maiden	1994	USA, GB, France	Behind The Scenes Ltd, Mount/Kramer, Channel 4 Films, Flach Film, Canal+, TF1, Capitol Films	02/01/1997
Shallow Grave	1994	GB	Channel Four Television, Glasgow Film Fund, Figment Films, Film Four International, Glasgow Film Fund	09/01/1997
Amateur	1994	GB, France, USA	Zenith Productions, UGC Images, True Fiction Pictures, American Playhouse, Public Broadcasting Service, Corporation for Public Broadcasting, National Endowment for the Arts, Chubb Group of Insurance Companies, U.G.C., American Playhouse Theatrical Films, La Sept Cinéma, Channel 4 Films, Sony Pictures Classics	16/01/1997
The Baby of Mâcon	1993	GB, France, Belgium, Netherlands, United Germany	Allarts Ltd, UGC Images, Allarts Productions Benelux B.V., Allarts Enterprises, U.G.C., La Sept, Cine Electra II, Channel Four, Filmstiftung NRW, Canal+, Channel 4 Films	23/01/1997
Trainspotting	1995	GB	Channel Four Television Corporation, Figment Films, Noel Gay Motion Picture Company, Channel Four, Channel 4 Films, Film Finances Ltd	26/11/1997
Blue Juice	1995	GB, France	Skreba Film	03/12/1997
Sister, My Sister	1994	GB	Channel Four Television Corporation, NFH Productions, Film Four International, British Screen	10/12/1997
Beautiful Thing	1996	GB	World Productions, Channel Four	17/12/1997
Safe	1995	GB, USA	American Playhouse, Killer Films	21/12/1997
A Midsummer Night's Dream	1996	UK, Spain	Arts Council of England, Capitol Films, Edenwood, Film Four (listed as distributor)	26/12/1997

Le Confessional	1995	Canada (Quebec), GB, France	Cinémaginaire, Confessionnal, Enigma Films Ltd, Cinéa, Téléfilm Canada, Société Générale des Industries Culturelles du Québec, Quebec Government, European Co-Production Fund (UK), Channel 4 Films, Ministère de la Culture et de la Francophonie, CNC – Centre national de la cinématographie	27/12/1997
The Neon Bible	1994	GB, Spain, USA	Scala (Neon Bible) Limited, Channel Four Television Corporation, Scala Productions, Channel Four, Screen Partners, Iberoamericana Films, Academy Pictures, Three Rivers, Channel 4 Films, European Script Fund	14/03/1998
Frankie Starlight	1995	Ireland, France, USA, United Germany, GB	Ferndale Films	21/03/1998
Institute Benjamenta	1995	GB, Japan, United Germany	Channel Four, British Screen, Koninck, Image Forum, Pandora Filmproduktion	28/03/1998
Secrets and Lies	1996	GB	CiBy 2000, Thin Man	13/04/1998
Brassed Off	1996	GB, USA	Channel Four Television Corporation, Prominent Features, Miramax Films	25/05/1998
Crime Time	1996	GB, USA, United Germany	Focus Films, Pandora Filmproduktion, Trimark Pictures, Channel 4 Films, Kinowelt Filmproduktion, ARD, Degeto Film, Arts Council of England, Bayerische Film und Fernsehförderung, Eurimages Conseil de l'Europe, European Script Fund	26/07/1998
The Hollow Reed	1996	GB, United Germany, Spain	Scala Productions, Channel Four Television Corporation, Senator Film Produktion GmbH, Cía. Iberoamericana de TV	26/10/1998 (?)
The Pillow Book	1995	Netherlands, France, GB, Luxemburg	Kasander & Wigman Productions, Alpha Films, Woodline Films, Channel 4 Films, Le Studio Canal+, DeLux Productions S.A., Eurimages Conseil de l'Europe, Stichting Nederlands Fonds voor de Film	01/11/1998
Nothing Personal	1995	GB, Ireland	Channel Four, Little Bird Company Limited, Bord Scannán na hÉireann, British Screen	21/11/1998

The Life and Extraordinary Adventures of Private Ivan Chonkin	1994	GB, France, Italy, Czech Republic, Russia (Republic)	Portobello Pictures Ltd, MK2 ProductionsCanal+, La Sept Cinéma, CNC – Centre national de la cinématographie, Channel Four, European Co-Production Fund (UK), Fandango Produzione Cinematografica, Domenico PROCACCI, Cable Plus, Krátky Film (Praha), Studio 89, Studio TriTe, Eric ABRAHAM, Marin KARMITZ, Eckonomica & Filmova Agentura	27/11/1998
Jump the Gun	1996	GB, South Africa	Parallax Pictures, Xencat Pictures, Channel Four	01/12/1998
Kama Sutra	1996	India, GB, Japan, German Federal Republic	Mirabai Films, NDF International, Pony Canyon, Pandora Filmproduktion	04/12/1998
Carla's Song	1996	GB, United Germany, Spain	Parallax Pictures, Channel 4 Films, Road Movies Filmproduktion GmbH, Tornasol Films, ARD, Degeto Film, Alta Films, TVE Televisión Española, Filmstiftung NRW	07/12/1998
Trojan Eddie	1996	GB, Ireland	Channel Four, Initial Films, Stratford Productions, Bord Scannán na hÉireann, Irish Screen	21/12/1998
Remember Me?	1996	GB	Channel 4 Films, Talisman Films	25/12/1998
The Gambler	1997	GB, Netherlands, Hungary	Channel 4 Films, Trendraise Company, Channel Four Television Corporation, Gambler Productions, Hungry Eye Pictures, Objektiv Filmstúdió, KRO, Stichting Nederlands Fonds voor de Film, Stichting Co-productiefonds Binnenlandse Omroep, Eurimages Conseil de l'Europe, European Script Fund	26/12/1998
Alive and Kicking	1996	GB	Martin Pope Productions, Channel 4 Films, Channel Four Television Corporation	30/12/1998
True Blue	1996	GB	Channel Four Television Corporation, Film & General Productions, Rafford Films, Arts Council of England	10/01/1999
Portraits Chinois (shadow play)	1996	France, GB	IMA Films, UGC Images, France 2 Cinéma, Polar Productions, Canal+, Sofinergie 3, Sofinergie 4, European Co-Production Fund (UK), Channel 4 Films	25/01/1999

Le Tregua (*The Truce*)	1996	Italy, United Germany, France, Switzerland	3 Emme Cinematografica, UGC Images, T & C Film AG (Zurich), DaZu, Stéphan Films (Paris), Capitol Films, Channel 4 Films	08/04/1999
Bent	1996	GB, USA, Japan	Channel Four Television Corporation, Nippon Film Development & Finance, Channel 4 Films, Ask Kodansha Co., Arts Council of England, Sarah Radclyffe Productions	22/04/1999
Welcome to Sarajevo	1997	GB, USA	Channel Four Television Corporation, Miramax Films, Dragon Pictures, Happening Films	26/04/1999
The Winter Guest	1996	USA, GB	Pressman/Lipper Productions, Capitol Films, Fine Line Features, Channel 4 Films, Scottish Film Production Fund, Scottish Arts Council Lottery Fund	01/05/1999
A Life Less Ordinary	1997	GB	Life Less Limited, PolyGram Filmed Entertainment, Figment Films, Channel Four	16/07/1999
A Further Gesture	1996	GB, United Germany, Japan, Ireland	Channel Four Television Corporation, NDF International, Zephyr Films, Samson Films, Road Movies Dritte Produktionen, Pony Canyon, Bord Scannán na hÉireann, Eurimages Conseil de l'Europe, Filmstiftung NRW, European Script Fund	26/07/1999
Downtime	1997	GB, France	Scala Productions, Pilgrim Films, IMA Films, Channel Four, Pandora Cinema, Arts Council of England, The Moving Image Development Agency, Merseyside Film Production Fund, Sofinergie 4, National Lottery through the Arts Council of England	03/10/1999
The Slab Boys	1997	Scotland	Channel Four Television Corporation, Skreba Films, Scottish Arts Council, Arts Council of England, Glasgow Film Fund, Wanderlust Pictures	27/10/1999
The Proprietor	1996	GB, France, Turkey, USA	Merchant Ivory Productions Ltd, Ognon Pictures, Fez Production Filmcilik, Inc. Largo Entertainment, Canal+, Channel Four, Eurimages Conseil de l'Europe	03/11/1999

The Woodlanders	1997	GB	Channel Four Television Corporation, Pathé Productions Ltd, River Films, Channel 4 Films, Pathé Productions Ltd, Arts Council of England, National Lottery through the Arts Council of England	11/12/1999
Babymother	1998	GB	Channel 4 Films, Formation Films, Arts Council of England, National Lottery through the Arts Council of England	19/12/1999
The Disappearance of Finbar	1996	Ireland, GB, Sweden, France	First City Features, Samson Films, Victoria Film AB, Film Four International, Channel 4 Films, Pandora Cinema, Bord Scannán na hÉireann, Svenska Filminstitutet, Midnight Sun Film & Cultural Productions AB, Eurimages Conseil de l'Europe, European Script Fund	23/12/1999
Last Night	1998	Canada, France	Rhombus Media, Canadian Broadcasting Corporation, La Sept ARTE, Haut et Court, CTCPF, Téléfilm Canada, Equity Investment Program, Canadian Film or Video Production Tax Credit Programme	31/12/1999
Velvet Goldmine	1998	GB, USA	Channel Four, Velvet Goldmine Productions, Newmarket Capital LLC, Zenith Productions, Killer Films, Single Cell Pictures, Newmarket Capital Group, Goldwyn Films International, Channel 4 Films, Miramax Films	12/02/2000
Martha Meet Frank, Daniel and Laurence	1998	GB	Channel Four Television Corporation, Banshee, Channel 4 Films	19/02/2000
Elizabeth	1998	GB	Inc. PolyGram Filmed Entertainment, Working Title Films, PolyGram Filmed Entertainment, Channel 4 Films	08/04/2000
Vigo Passion for Life	1997	GB, Japan, France, Spain, United Germany	Impact Pictures, Nitrate Film Limited, MACT Productions, Channel 4 Films, Little Magic Films, Tornasol Films, Road Movies Vierte Produktionen, Canal+, WDR/ARTE, Channel Four Television Corporation, DML, Amuse Inc., TV Tokyo, European Script Fund	09/04/2000

Film	Year	Country	Production companies	Date
The Land Girls	1997	GB, France	Intermedia Land Girls Ltd, Caméra One, Aréna Films (Paris), InterMedia Films, The Greenlight Fund, Channel 4 Films, Greenpoint Films, West Eleven Films, National Lottery through the Arts Council of England	15/04/2000
Solomon and Gaenor	1998	Wales	Sianel Pedwar Cymru, Film Four Distributors, Arts Council of England, Cyngor Celfyddydau Cymru/Arts Council of Wales, APT Film and Television, September Films, National Lottery through the Arts Council of England, National Lottery through the Arts Council of Wales	26/04/2000
Career Girls	1997	GB	Channel Four Television Corporation, Thin Man Films, Matrix Film Partnership	12/05/2000
Croupier	1997	GB	Channel 4, British Film Institute	N/A
My Name is Joe	1998	GB, United Germany, France, Italy, Spain	Parallax (Joe) Ltd, Road Movies Vierte Produktionen, Parallax Pictures, Scottish Arts Council Lottery Fund, Glasgow Film Fund, Filmstiftung NRW, Channel 4 Films, WDR – Westdeutscher Rundfunk, ARTE, La Sept Cinéma, ARD, Degeto Film, BIM Distribuzione, Diaphana Films, Tornasol Films Alta Films	08/07/2000
Dancing at Lughnasa	1998	Ireland, GB, USA	Ferndale Films, Lenrey Ltd, Capitol Films, Sony Pictures Classics, Channel 4 Films, Bord Scannán na hÉireann, Radio-Telefís Éireann, Pandora Cinema, Samson Films	21/07/2000
Food of Love	1997	GB, France	Channel Four Television Corporation, MP Productions, Film Four Distributors, Film Four International, Intrinsica Films, Channel 4 Films, Arts Council of England, Canal+	07/08/2000
Endurance	1998	USA, GB	La Junta, Hollywood Pictures Company, Film Four Limited, Helkon Medien AG	03/09/2000
The Boys	1998	Australia, GB	Arenafilm, Axiom Films Limited, Australian Film Commission, The Premium Movie Partnership, SBS Independent, Australian Film Finance Corporation, New South Wales Film and Television Office	10/09/2000

Hilary and Jackie	1998	GB	Oxford Film Company, Film Four Limited, InterMedia Film Equities, InterMedia Films, British Screen, Arts Council of England, National Lottery through the Arts Council of England, European Script Fund, BBC	23/09/2000
Prometheus	1998	GB	Film Four Limited, Holmes Associates, Arts Council of England, National Lottery through the Arts Council of England	24/09/2000
Orphans	1997	GB	Channel Four Television Corporation, Channel 4 Films, Scottish Arts Council Lottery Fund, Glasgow Film Fund, Antonine Green Bridge, Scottish Film Production Fund	30/09/2000

Bibliography

Primary and archival sources

British Film Institute Special Collections

BFI Special Collections, Papers of Roger Graef, CF Paper 215 (February 1984).
BFI Special Collections, Papers of Roger Graef, CF Paper 312, 'Film on Four' (1985).
BFI Special Collections, Papers of Roger Graef, CF Paper 313, 'Commissioning editors' work loads' (1985).

British Universities Film and Video Council

Channel 4 Television, Channel 4 Press Information Packs, Season Information Pack (Spring 1987).
Channel 4 Television, Channel 4 Press Information Packs, 1989/90, week 49.
Channel 4 Television, Channel 4 Press Information Packs, 1991, week 18.
Channel 4 Television, Channel 4 Press Information Packs, Season Information Pack (Winter 1993).
Channel 4 Television, Channel 4 Press Information Channel 4 Press Packs, Season Information Pack (Autumn 1995).
Channel 4 Television, Channel 4 Press Information Packs, Season Information Pack (Autumn 1997).

Reports, policy documents and official publications

British Screen Advisory Council, *Report on Activities 1 January 1986 to 31 May 1987* (London: BSAC, 1987).

British Screen Finance Limited, 'Accounts for the Year Ended 31 December 1986' (London: British Screen Finance, 1986).

Channel 4 Television, *Annual Report and Accounts* (London: Channel 4 Television Corporation, 1987).

Channel 4 Television, 'This is Channel 4' (London: Channel 4, 1994).

Deloitte and Touche, *The Cost of Making Dreams: Accounting for the British Film Industry* (London: BFI, 1999).

House of Commons, Cmnd. 6753-I, *Home Office: Report of the Committee on the Future of Broadcasting*, London, 1976–1977.

House of Commons, National Heritage Committee, 'The British Film Industry: Second Report', Vol. 1 (1995).

Narval Media, *Stories We Tell Ourselves: The Cultural Impact of UK Film 1946–2006* (London: UKFC, 2009).

Northern Alliance and Ipsos MediaCT, *Opening Our Eyes: How Film Contributes to the Culture of the UK* (London: BFI, 2001).

Oldsberg SPI, *Channel 4's Contribution to the UK Film Sector* (London: Oldsberg, 2008).

Secondary sources

Books

Abbott, Stacey, ed., *Falling in Love Again: Romantic Comedy in Contemporary Cinema* (London: I. B. Tauris, 2009).

Ashby, Justine and Higson, Andrew, *British Cinema, Past and Present* (London: Routledge, 2000).

Auty, Martyn and Roddick, Nick, eds, *British Cinema Now* (London: BFI, 1985).

Beck, Andrew, ed., *Cultural Work: Understanding the Cultural Industries* (London: Routledge, 2003).

Berra, John, *Declarations of Independence: American Cinema and the Partiality of Independent Production* (Chicago: Intellect, 2008).

Bignell, Jonathan and Lacey, Stephen, eds, *British Television Drama: Past, Present and Future* (Basingstoke: Palgrave, 2000).

Bilton, Chris, *Management and Creativity: From Creative Industries to Creative Management* (Oxford: Blackwell, 2007).

Biskind, Peter, *Down and Dirty Pictures: Miramax, Sundance and the Rise of Independent Film* (London: Bloomsbury, 2004).

Blaney, Martin, *Symbiosis or Confrontation? The Relationship Between the Film Industry and Television in the Federal Republic of Germany from 1950 to 1985* (Berlin: Edition Sigma, 1992).

Bonner, Paul, with Aston, Leslie, *Independent Television in Britain Volume 6: New Developments in Independent Television, 1981–92: Channel 4, TV-am, Cable and Satellite* (Basingstoke: Palgrave, 2003).

Bourdieu, Pierre, *The Field of Cultural Production* (Oxford: Polity Press, 1993).

Brandt, George, ed., *British Television Drama in the 1980s* (Cambridge: Cambridge University Press, 1993).

Brown, Maggie, *A Licence to Be Different: The Story of Channel 4* (London: BFI Publishing, 2007).

Cashmore, Ellis, *. . . and Then There Was Television* (London: Routledge, 1994).

Catterall, Peter, *The Making of Channel 4* (London: Frank Cass, 1998).

Caughie, John, *Television Drama: Realism, Modernism, and British Culture* (Oxford: Oxford University Press, 2000).

Chapman, James, *Past and Present: National Identity and the British Historical Film* (London: I. B. Tauris, 2005).

Chapman, James, Harper, Sue and Glancy, Mark, eds, *The New Film History: Sources, Methods, Approaches* (Hampshire: Palgrave Macmillan, 2007).

Cooke, Lez, *British Television Drama* (London: BFI Publishing, 2003).

Coveney, Michael, *The World According to Mike Leigh* (London: Harper Collins, 1996).

Crissel, Andrew, *An Introductory History of British Broadcasting* 2nd edn (London: Routledge, 2005).

Dale, Martin, *The Movie Game: Film Business in Britain, Europe and America* (New York: Continuum International Publishing Group Ltd, 1997).

Darlow, Michael, *Independents Struggle: The Programme Makers Who Took on the TV Establishment* (London: Boa Ms Ltd, 2004).

Dave, Paul, *Visions of England: Class and Culture in Contemporary Cinema* (Oxford: Bloomsbury, 2006).

De Valck, Marijke, *Film Festivals: From European Geopolitics to Global Cinephilia* (Amsterdam: Amsterdam University Press, 2007).

Elsaesser, Thomas, *European Cinema: Face to Face with Hollywood* (Amsterdam: Amsterdam University Press, 2005).

Ezra, Elizabeth and Rowden, Terry, eds, *Transnational Cinema, the Film Reader* (London: Routledge, 2006).

Finney, Angus, *The Egos Have Landed: The Rise and Fall of Palace Pictures* (London: William Heinemann Ltd, 1996).

Fowler, Catherine and Helfield, Gillian, eds, *Representing the Rural: Space, Place and Identity in Films about the Land* (Detroit: Wayne State University Press, 2006).

Friedman, Lester, ed., *Fires Were Started: British Cinema and Thatcherism*, 2nd edn (Minneapolis: Minnesota University Press, 1993).

Fuller, Graham, *Loach on Loach* (London: Faber and Faber, 1998).

Galt, Rosalind, *The New European Cinema: Redrawing the Map* (New York: Colombia University Press, 2006).

Geraghty, Christine, *My Beautiful Laundrette* (New York: I. B. Tauris, 2004).

Harcourt, Amanda, *The Independent Producer: Film and Television* (London: Faber & Faber, 1986).

Harper, Graeme and Rayner, Jonathan, *Cinema and Landscape: Film, Nation and Cultural Geography* (Chicago: University of Chicago Press).

Hayward, Anthony, *Which Side Are You On? Ken Loach and his Films* (London: Bloomsbury, 2004).

Hesmondhalgh, David, *The Cultural Industries* (London: Sage, 2002).

Higson, Andrew, *English Heritage, English Cinema* (Oxford: Oxford University Press, 2003).

Hill, John, *British Cinema in the 1980s: Issues and Themes* (Oxford: Clarendon Press, 1999).

Hill, John, *Ken Loach: The Politics of Film and Television* (London: BFI, 2011).

Hill, John and McLoone, Martin, eds, *Big Picture, Small Screen: The Relations Between Film and Television* (Luton: University of Luton Press, 1996).

Hilmes, Michele, ed., *The Television History Book* (London: BFI Publishing, 2003).

Hobson, Dorothy, *Channel 4: The Early Years and the Jeremy Isaacs Legacy* (London: I. B. Tauris, 2007).

Hood, Stuart, ed., *Behind the Screens: The Structure of British Television in the Nineties* (London: Lawrence and Wishart, 1994).

Isaacs, Jeremy, *Storm Over 4: A Personal Account* (London: Weidenfeld & Nicolson, 1989).

Jacobs, Jason and Peacock, Stephen, eds, *Television Aesthetics and Style* (London: Bloomsbury, 2013).

Johnson, Catherine, *Branding Television* (London: Routledge, 2012).

King, Geoff, *Indiewood, USA: Where Hollywood Meets Independent Cinema* (New York: I. B. Tauris, 2009).

Kuhn, Michael, *One Hundred Films and a Funeral: The Life and Death of PolyGram Films* (London: Thorogood, 2003).

Lay, Samantha, *British Social Realism: From Documentary to Brit-grit* (London: Wallflower Press, 2002).

Mather, Nigel, *Tears of Laughter: Comedy Drama in 1990s British Cinema* (Manchester: Manchester University Press, 2006).

Medley, Nick and Woodward, John, *Productive Relationships?* (London: BFI, 1991).

Murphy, Robert, ed., *British Cinema of the 1990s* (London: BFI Publishing, 2000).

Murphy, Robert, ed., *The British Cinema Book*, 2nd edn (London: BFI Publishing, 2001).

Paterson, Richard, ed., *The Broadcasting Debate 1* (London: BFI Publishing, 1990).

Petrie, Duncan, *Creativity and Constraint in the British Film Industry* (London: Macmillan, 1991).

Petrie, Duncan, ed., *Inside Stories: Diaries of British Filmmakers at Work* (London: BFI Publishing, 1996).

Petrie, Duncan, ed., *New Questions of British Cinema* (London: BFI, 1992).

Potter, Ian, *The Rise and Rise of Independents* (Isleworth: Guerilla Books, 2008).

Pym, John, *Film on Four: A Survey 1982–1991* (London: BFI, 1992).

Raphael, Amy, *Danny Boyle: In His Own Words* (London: Faber and Faber, 2011).

Rolinson, David, *Alan Clarke* (Manchester: Manchester University Press, 2005).

Sargeant, Amy, *British Cinema: A Critical History* (London: BFI Publishing, 2005).

Scriven, Michael and Lecomte, Monia, eds, *Television Broadcasting in Contemporary France and Britain* (New York: Berghahn Books, 1999).

Spicer, Andrew and McKenna, Anthony, eds, *Beyond the Bottom Line: The Producer in Film and Television Studies* (London: Bloomsbury Academic, 2014).

Street, Sarah, *British National Cinema* (Oxford: Taylor and Francis, 1997).

Street, Sarah, *Transatlantic Crossings: British Feature Films in the USA* (London: Continuum, 2002).

Taylor, Barnaby F., *The British New Wave* (Manchester: Manchester University Press, 2006).

Walker, Alexander, *Icons in the Fire: The Rise and Fall of Practically Everyone in the British Film Industry 1984–2000* (London: Orion, 2004).

West Midlands Arts, *Films and Plays from Pebble Mill: Ten Years of Regional Television Drama* (Stafford: West Midlands Arts, 1980).

Wheatley, Helen, ed., *Re-viewing Television History: Critical Issues in Television Historiography* (London: I. B. Tauris, 2007).

Wickham, Phil, *Producing the Goods? UK Film Production, 1991–2001* (London: BFI, 2002).

Wickham, Phil, *Back to the Future: The Fall and Rise of the British Film Industry in the 1980s* (London: BFI, 2005).

Williams, Christopher, ed., *Cinema: The Beginnings and the Future* (London: University of Westminster Press, 1996).

de Winter, Helen, *'What I Really Want to do is Produce …': Top Producers Talk Movies and Money* (London: Faber & Faber, 2006).

Working Title, *Laundrettes and Lovers: From Storyboard to Billboard* (London: Boxtree Ltd, 2003).

Chapters in edited books

Auty, Martyn, 'But Is It cinema?', in *British Cinema Now*, ed. by Martyn Auty and Nick Roddick (London: BFI, 1985), 57–70.

Barr, Charles, 'They Think it's all Over: The Dramatic Legacy of Live Television', in *Big Picture, Small Screen: The Relations Between Film and Television*, ed. by John Hill and Martin McLoone (Luton: University of Luton Press, 1996), 47–75.

Berkeley, Dina, 'Creativity and Economic Transactions in TV Drama', in *Cultural Work: Understanding the Cultural Industries*, ed. by Andrew Beck (London: Routledge, 2003), 103–20.

Caughie, John 'The Logic of Convergence', in *Big Picture, Small Screen: The Relations Between Film and Television*, ed. by John Hill and Martin McLoone (Luton: University of Luton Press, 1996), 215–23.

Ellis, John, 'Innovation in Form and Content?', in *The Television History Book*, ed. by Michele Hilmes (London: BFI Publishing, 2003), 95–8.

Giles, Paul, 'History with Holes: Channel 4 Television Films of the 1980s', in *Fires Were Started: British Cinema and Thatcherism*, ed. by Lester Friedman, 2nd edn (Minneapolis: Minnesota University Press, 1993), 58–74.

Grade, Michael, 'Getting the Right Approach', in *Big Picture, Small Screen: The Relations Between Film and Television*, ed. by John Hill and Martin McLoone (Luton: University of Luton Press, 1996), 177–82.

Hanson, Barry, 'The 1970s: Regional Variations', in *British Television Drama: Past, Present and Future*, ed. by Jonathan Bignell et al. (Basingstoke: Palgrave, 2000), 166–71.

Harvey, Sylvia 'Channel 4 Television: From Annan to Grade', in *Behind the Screens: The Structure of British Television in the Nineties*, ed. by Stuart Hood (London: Lawrence & Wishart, 1999), 102–32.

Higson, Andrew, 'A Green and Pleasant Land: Rural Spaces and British Cinema', in *Representing the Rural: Space, Place and Identity in Films about the Land*, ed. by Catherine Fowler and Gillian Helfield (Detroit: Wayne State University Press, 2006), 240–58.

Higson, Andrew, 'The Instability of the National', in *British Cinema, Past and Present*, ed. by Andrew Higson and Justine Ashby (London: Routledge, 2000), 35–48.

Higson, Andrew, 'The Limiting Imagination of National Cinema', in *Transnational Cinema, the Film Reader*, ed. by Elizabeth Ezra and Terry Rowden (London, Routledge, 2006), 15–25.

Hill, John, 'British Television and Film: The Making of a Relationship?', in *Big Picture, Small Screen: The Relations Between Film and Television*, ed. by John Hill and Martin McLoone (Luton: University of Luton Press, 1996), 151–76.

Hill, John, 'From the New Wave to Brit Grit: Continuity and Difference in Working-Class Realism', in *British Cinema, Past and Present*, ed. by Andrew Higson and Justine Ashby (London: Routledge, 2000), 249–60.

Honess Roe, Annabel, 'A "Special Relationship?" The Coupling of Britain and America in Working Title's Romantic Comedies', in *Falling in Love Again: Romantic Comedy in Contemporary Cinema*, ed. by Stacey Abbott (London: I. B. Tauris, 2009), 77–88.

Jäckel, Anne, 'Broadcaster's Involvement in Co-Productions', in *Television Broadcasting in Contemporary France and Britain*, ed. by Michael Scriven and Monia Lecomte (New York: Berghahn Books, 1999), 175–97.

James, Annie Morgan, 'Enchanted Places, Land and Sea, and Wilderness: Scottish Highland Landscape and Identity in Cinema', in *Representing the Rural: Space, Place and Identity in Films about the Land*, ed. by Catherine Fowler and Gillian Helfield (Detroit: Wayne State University Press, 2006), 185–201.

James, Nick, 'They Think It's All Over: British Cinema's US Surrender', in *The British Cinema Book*, ed. by Robert Murphy, 2nd edn (London: BFI Publishing, 2002), 302–7.

McLoone, Martin, 'Boxed in? The Aesthetics of Film and Television', in *Big Picture, Small Screen: The Relations Between Film and Television*, ed. by John Hill and Martin McLoone (Luton: University of Luton Press, 1996), 76–106.

McLoone, Martin, 'Landscape in Irish Cinema', in *Cinema and Landscape: Film, Nation and Cultural Geography*, ed. by Graeme Harper and Jonathan Rayner (Chicago: University of Chicago Press), 131–46.

Paterson, Richard, 'Changing Conditions of Independent Production in the UK', in *New Questions of British Cinema*, ed. by Duncan Petrie (London: BFI Publishing, 1991), 40–8.

Spark, Colin, 'Independent Production, Unions, and Casualisation', in *Behind the Screens: The Structure of British Television in the Nineties*, ed. by Stuart Hood (London: Lawrence & Wishart, 1999), 133–54.

Spicer, Andrew, 'The Independent Producer and the State: Simon Relph, Government Policy and the British Film Industry, 1980–2005', in *Beyond the Bottom Line: The Producer in Film and Television Studies* ed. by Andrew Spicer and Anthony McKenna (London: Bloomsbury Academic, 2014), 65–93.

Spicer, Andrew, 'Part II – Authorship', in *The New Film History: Sources, Methods, Approaches*, ed. by James Chapman, Sue Harper and Mark Glancy (Hampshire: Palgrave Macmillan, 2007), 69–71.

Williams, Christopher, 'The Social Art Cinema: A Moment in the History of British Film and Television Culture', in *Cinema: The Beginnings and the Future*, ed. by Christopher Williams (London: University of Westminster Press, 1996), 190–200.

Journal articles

Allen, Michael P. and Lincoln, Anne E., 'Critical Discourse and the Cultural Consecration of American Films', *Social Forces*, 82:3 (2004), 871–94.
Aylett, Holly, 'Reflections on the Cultural Value of Film', *Journal of British Cinema and Television*, 2:2 (2005), 343–51.
Blair, Helen, 'Working in Film: Employment in a Project Based Industry', *Personnel Review*, 30:2 (2001), 170–85.
Brunsdon, Charlotte, '"It's a Film": Medium Specificity as Textual Gesture in Red Road and The Unloved', *Journal of British Cinema and Television*, 9:3 (2012), 457–79.
Durmaz, Bahar, Platt, Stephen and Yigitcanlar, Tan, 'Creativity, Culture Tourism and Place-making: Istanbul and London Film Industries', *International Journal of Culture, Tourism and Hospitality*, 4:3 (2010), 198–213.
Ellis, John, 'Channel 4: Working Notes', *Screen*, 24:6 (1983), 37–51.
Higson, Andrew, 'Space, Place, Spectacle', *Screen*, 25:4–5 (1984), 2–21.
Lampel, Joseph, 'Classics Foretold? Contemporaneous and Retrospective Consecration in the UK Film Industry', *Cultural Trends*, 18:3 (2009), 239–48.
Long, Christopher, 'Revising the Film Canon', *New Review of Film and Television Studies*, 4:1 (2006), 17–35.
McIntyre, Steve, 'New Images of Scotland', *Screen*, 25:1 (1984), 53–60.
Revall, Eva, 'A Systems View of Film-making as a Creative Practice', *Northern Lights: Film and Media Studies Yearbook*, 10:1 (2012), 57–73.
Roberts, James Paul, 'Revisiting the Creative/Commercial Clash: An Analysis of Decision-Making During Product Development in the Television Industry', *Media Culture Society*, 32:5 (2010), 761–92.
Spicer, Andrew, 'Creativity and Commerce: Michael Klinger and New Film History', *New Review of Film and Television Studies*, 8:3 (2010), 297–314.
Spicer, Andrew, 'Debate: The Cultural Value of UK Film Report on a Seminar Held at Senate House, University of London, 3 May 2005', *Journal of British Cinema and Television*, 2:2 (2005), 338–43.
Staiger, Janet, 'The Politics of Film Canons', *Cinema Journal*, 24:3 (1985), 4–23.
Turok, Ivan, 'Cities, Clusters and Creative Industries: The Case of Film and Television in Scotland', *European Planning Studies*, 11:5 (2003), 549–65.

Newspaper, magazine articles and reviews

Adair, Gilbert, 'Review: *Another Time Another Place*', *Monthly Film Bulletin* (August 1983).
Anon., 'A Year of Living Differently', *Time Out*, 27 November 1983.
Anon., 'Another Time, Another Place', *Stills* (July 1983).

Anon., 'C4 pledges an extra 4m for feature film investment', *Screen International*, 5 May 1995.

Anon., 'Channel 4 Face Dilemma', *Broadcast*, 1 February 1985.

Anon., 'Darlow Film on Four for next season', *Stage* (July 1983).

Anon., 'Grade vows to fight on over C4 funding formula', *Screen Finance*, 25 January 1995.

Anon., 'Interview with Stephen Woolley', *Premiere* (April 1993).

Anon., 'Jeremy Isaacs Reports Back', *AIP&Co*, 48 (1983).

Anon., 'Palace Through the Looking Glass?', *Screen International*, 7 May 1992.

Appleyard, Bryan, 'Children of Channel 4', *Sunday Times Magazine*, 21 February 1988.

Bennett, Ronan, 'Lean, Mean, and Cruel', *Sight and Sound*, 5:1 (January 1995).

Brown, Hilary, 'The Film Man', *Airwaves*, 13 (Winter 1987/88).

Coles, Joanna, 'Life in the Small Frame', *The Guardian*, 18 May 1993.

Coyne, Larry, 'TV used to feed off the cinema, now the reverse is true', *Broadcast*, 9 May 1986.

Dawtrey, Adam, 'Screen's Siren Song Lures Brit Legiters', *Variety*, 12–18 December 1994.

Dowling, Tim, 'Curtis Britain: A Brief Guide', *The Guardian*, 13 November 2003.

Finney, Angus, 'New Crew in Uncharted Waters', *Screen International*, 1 March 1991.

Fraser, Nicholas, 'Small No Longer Beautiful on 4', *The Observer*, 4 February 1990.

Gristwood, Sarah, 'Trendspotting: Four's Shot in the Arm for New Movies', *The Independent*, 19 December 1997.

Hassan, Mamoun et al., 'Life Before Death on Television', *Sight and Sound*, 53:2 (Spring 1984).

Hayward, Anthony, 'Producers at loggerheads over Films on Four', *Screen International*, 25 June 1983.

Isaacs, Jeremy, 'Happy Birthday to the Leader with the Golden Touch', *The Independent*, 8 November 2004.

Isaacs, Jeremy, 'Letter from the Chief Executive', *4 This Month* (November 1982).

Jackson, Kevin, 'When Every Second Counts', *The Independent*, 8 February 1993.

Kerr, Paul, 'The British with their Trousers Down', *The Listener*, 28 August 1986.

KM, 'C4 Film Wait', *Broadcast*, 4 October 1982.

Lambert, Stephen, 'Still Smiling: An Interview with Jeremy Isaacs', *Stills*, 6 (May–June 1983).

Malcolm, Derek, 'The Pursuit of Innocents', *Guardian Weekly*, 14 August 1983.

O'Connor, John, 'Accounts', *New York Times*, 4 July 1986.

Pym, John, 'Showman Grade Boosts Ratings, Riles Critics', *Screen International*, 11 November 1992.

Quart, Leonard, 'Review: *Letter to Brezhnev*', *Cineaste*, 15:1 (1986).

Quart, Leonard, 'Review: *Sammy and Rosie Get Laid*', *Cineaste*, 16:4 (1987).

Reevel, Philip, 'Films, Four, and Funding', *Televisual* (February 1985).

Robinson, David, 'A Year of Film on Four – and After', *4 This Month*, 2 (December 1983).

Salewicz, Chris, 'Moscow on the Mersey', *Time Out* (Oct/Dec 1985).

Saynor, James, 'Writers' Television', *Sight and Sound*, 2:7 (November 1992).

Stuart, Andrea, 'Blackpool Illumination', *Sight and Sound*, 4:2 (February 1994).

Taylor, Sebastian, 'C4 sales on target to reach 4m', *Broadcast*, 28 November 1986.

Wade, Graham, 'Powell's Picture Palace', *Stills* (March 1985).

Websites

http://awards.bafta.org
http://bufvc.ac.uk
http://news.bbc.co.uk
http://www.empireonline.com
http://www.film4.com
http://www.guerilla-films.com
www.imbd.com
http://www.listal.com
http://www.telegraph.co.uk
http://www.timeout.com

Unpublished material

Andrews, Hannah, 'Public service broadcasters and British cinema, 1990–2010' (doctoral book, University of Warwick, 2011).

Chan, Felicia and Willis, Andrew, 'Missed, Lost and Forgotten Opportunities: *Ping Pong* and *Soursweet*', conference paper presented at the Channel 4 and British Film Culture Conference, BFI Southbank, 1 November 2012.

EU Authorised Representative:

Easy Access System Europe Mustamäe tee 50, 10621 Tallinn, Estonia

gpsr.requests@easproject.com

Printed and bound by CPI Group (UK) Ltd, Croydon, CR0 4YY

12/05/2026

02108441-0002